CREATED TO RELATE

CREATED TO RELATE

Living Beyond Religion

Desiree Taylor

Carpenter's Son Publishing

Created to Relate: Living Beyond Religion

Published by Carpenter's Son Publishing, Franklin, Tennessee
Carpenterssonpublishing.com

Edited by Gail Fallen

Cover and Interior Design by Suzanne Lawing

Printed in the United States of America

ISBN: 978-1-956370-44-7 (print)

This book is dedicated to my husband, Duane,
the one who has lived this journey with me.
My best friend, love of my life, and my biggest supporter.

FOREWORD

I grew up a "good girl." I figured out early on that I would get the attention, affirmation, and affection I desperately wanted by becoming the one who obeyed and colored inside the lines. I knew all the verses, I prayed all the prayers, people came to me for advice, and they always knew I was the one who they could count on to serve.

We all have a deep need for an identity, one that is rooted, something that tells us who we are and how we should feel about ourselves. Some may craft their identity around being a mother, others a student, or some a wife. These things aren't merely roles to play or obligations to fulfill; they become where we look to get our value. Mine was being a good Christian girl.

There is nothing wrong with any of these things. Being a great wife, mother, student, or Christian is admirable, yet they cannot give us our value. They cannot define us; only Jesus can do that. And we can notice where our identity truly lies and where we have been looking to tell us we're okay by how we react when it's removed from our lives.

Over my own long process, I discovered that my identity wasn't in Christ but in what I did for Him. When I wasn't able to check the boxes, and no one was patting me on the back for all the good deeds I had done, I withered. If the church, church leadership, or my own spirituality couldn't give me the validation I needed and craved, I began to wonder what purpose I could find at all.

Through a season of deep depression and anxiety, all my validating places seemed stripped from me. I could no longer perform, and with nothing to give but brokenness and tears, I was faced with what I really believed. What was God doing, and why was He allowing it? I thought that doing all the "right things" earned my spot in God's love and favor. Why on earth was He allowing this crushing, this wrestling? Nothing made sense anymore. The only thing I had left was the question, "Does God love me even when I have nothing to offer?"

If I am honest, I had always pictured God frustrated and impatiently tapping His foot with folded arms, waiting for me to get it together. But I believe He allowed this season in my life to show me that even in my ashes, He was there. He was not shaming or scolding me like I feared; He was loving me and helping me release the lies I had believed. His purpose was always to show me my one and true identity was in Him alone.

Desiree and I both know this path well; it is the journey God graciously brings those who dare to travel it. *Created to Relate* is the gentle companion with you on that journey from someone who has been there. Desiree gently unfolds each step, how God revealed it in her life, and why it is so very important. As you travel with her in these pages, let the Lord do what He has come to do. His path may not always be easy, but it always ends with the greatest gifts. He is so worthy.

Ashley Morgan Jackson, author of *Tired of Trying*

CONTENTS

Introduction 15

Chapter 1: A Deep Ache 21

Chapter 2: Take Me in Your Arms: From Judge to Father 27

Chapter 3: Dancing for an Audience of One 33

Chapter 4: The Love Letter of God's Word 41

Chapter 5: Prayer: Transformation from Acquaintance to Friend 51

Chapter 6: Learning Who I Am through the Eyes of Jesus 61

Chapter 7: Watching the Relational Walls Fall Down 71

Chapter 8: From the Building to the Body 81

Chapter 9: Being Brought Back to the Heart of Worship 91

Chapter 10: Leaving the Pharisee Life and Loving Those Left Behind 99

Chapter 11: The Cost of Freedom to Follow Jesus . . 109

Chapter 12: Moving Forward with a Transformed Heart 119

Acknowledgments. 129

About the Author 131

Notes. 133

INTRODUCTION

I have attended church for as long as I can remember. When I reminisce, I think about being a young girl dressed up in my proper church attire, sitting with my mom and sister in the same pew we settled into each week. My mom was deaf, and I had progressive hearing loss, so we would always sit up front where my mom's friend Betty would interpret the music and service for us. What a blessing that was to my mom and me. If not for Betty's kindness and willingness to use the gift God had given her, we wouldn't have been able to participate in the service very well at all.

After settling into our seats, I would begin to position myself, sitting up straight and tall and crossing my legs, longing to be noticed and acknowledged as a grown-up or at least as someone mature enough to receive communion. After all, only adults received communion, and the young were to be seen and not heard.

I was taught the importance of reading Scripture and having daily devotional and prayer time with God. Oddly, I didn't always see those around me living that way. I found out later that some people kept this time private, so no one really knew about it or saw it happening. I didn't hear much about Jesus in church, at least not in a relational way. We would hear about Him in popular Bible stories or in a general way in a sermon or Bible study.

I don't have any recollection of anyone sharing about their own personal relationship with Jesus outside of salvation until later in life. Again, this seemed to be what was taught; relationships were kept private and not talked about at all. The Holy Spirit was a complete stranger altogether. High school Bible class consisted of learning about all the don'ts of sex, drugs, and alcohol without much guidance on how actually to live that out in real life.

When I was nine, I first accepted Jesus into my heart. I had been attending a Baptist church, and I had friends and schoolmates who were part of another denomination. As I listened at my church and then heard friends and schoolmates talk about their churches and lives, I noticed differences in what they said and believed about God. What I was learning didn't always match up, and I began asking God, "Who are You?"

That began my journey with God, with me asking Him many questions and seeking to understand who He is. After asking questions and searching for a little while, I realized in my own heart that I was a sinner and needed a Savior, Jesus Christ, the Son of the living God. This truth became real to me, and I repented of my sins and invited Jesus into my heart. I still had many questions, and the journey with God was just beginning.

Soon after, I was baptized, and my relationship with Jesus moved to another level. I could tell something had changed in me, but I didn't understand it. All the requirements to be a good Christian that I was taught previously would scroll through my head like a Rolodex. (For my younger readers, imagine a spindle with rotating business cards attached to it in alphabetical order—extremely popular from the late 1950s through the 1990s.) In my head, my Rolodex cards would read, *Make sure you do your devotions and be in God's Word. Say your prayers. Obey your parents.* The list went on and on. There would also be cards listing everything and everyone I should stay away from. When I didn't do these things, I felt guilty and tried harder to do better. But it just became a checkbox of dos and don'ts with no real purpose.

Doing things just to check them off a list causes them to lose meaning. The actions become robotic, and the process starts to get exhausting.

After trying to live this out as a teenager with hearing loss and struggling to make friends, I began feeling isolated. I already felt different because of my hearing loss, and when I became a Christian, I thought I stood out even more. Life felt extremely hard and very lonely.

One day, I looked around, and it seemed other teenagers had lots of friends, nice clothes, and wonderful lives. Everything appeared to be going so well for all of them, and they weren't Christians. The grass began looking much greener on the other side.

Doubts filled my heart and mind, and I gave in to my struggle, pain, and doubts by taking a break from God.

It wasn't long before I found myself in a dark place, and God met me there in a personal way. One night, I broke down in tears and began to pray genuinely for the first time in a long time. As I closed my eyes, I saw a vision of Jesus reaching His hand down to me in the deep, dark pit I had found myself in. God spoke to my heart and asked me to reach for His hand. He said He would lift me out of that pit if I let Him and if I willingly reached out to Him.

I reached out my hand that night, and God was faithful.

True to His character, God brings good things out of bad places. He blessed me with my oldest son, Kyle. God used this beautiful boy's life to show me unconditional love and to give me a renewed purpose and desire to become a better person.

I repented and turned back to God, and my relationship with Jesus became more real. Until now, it had just been Kyle and me as a family unit, and I wanted to concentrate on being a mother and getting myself back to a healthier place. One night, I came to a place where I told God I would be content with just Him and Kyle for the rest of my life. I no longer wanted to chase after the wrong things or seek the wrong people in order to be loved.

Not long after, God brought my husband, Duane, and I together, and with Kyle, we became a family. We were married, and a few years later, I became a mother again to our second son, David. Even though I had grown, I still struggled with the Rolodex cards in my mind. I battled with trying to measure up as a good wife, mom, and Christian woman.

I failed at being in God's Word daily and struggled with memorizing Scripture. And my prayer life sounded more like desperate pleas and grocery shopping lists. Trying to keep up with two young boys but being unable to hear them, I found myself burning meals and not keeping the house in the condition I thought it should be. I couldn't do things while listening to the boys in the other room; I had to see them to make sure they were safe. So many nights I was beyond exhausted, and I struggled with loving everyone in my household well, including myself.

One day, I was completely spent and unable to do it anymore. I just broke down and released my feelings of inadequacy and failure to the Lord. I heard Him speak gently to my heart, "You are trying to earn what I have already given to you." He revealed to me that I was trying to earn God's love with my actions, and I was stuck in a pattern of works, but He loved me exactly where I was.

I had been living my Christian life like a daily to-do list. I was literally making lists of what I needed to do. I checked off tasks once I did them, or I left them blank if I didn't do them. Many days, I felt like a failure, living under the rubble of condemnation and shame. I was empty with nothing to offer God or anyone else around me, yet I still kept trying to earn a right standing with God. Even though my heart was in the right place, I had never understood that God wanted a relationship with me. My striving could never make me what I needed to be. Instead, God had sent His Son, Jesus Christ, to die, then raised Him from the dead to live again so that my relationship with Him could be restored beyond the dos and don'ts.

This is how God loved me and how much God loves you!

This day was the beginning of a lifelong journey for me. It has not been a short or easy ride, to say the least. I have repeatedly experienced a defeated mindset that needed to be renewed. I've also had to unlearn incorrect ideas about God that I learned over the years. I began to look at God's Word and prayer differently and face what I didn't know about the Holy Spirit. I had to learn that God loves and accepts me, not because of what I did or didn't do but because

I am His. I had to learn how to genuinely trust the love God was offering me.

I don't know where you are from or where you have been, but I pray that God uses my testimony to show you that you were created for a relationship with Him and that there is life beyond a vicious religious cycle like the one I experienced.

I encourage you to join me as I share this personal journey with you, and I pray Jesus becomes real to you and that you walk away knowing and believing His love for you. I pray you will be filled with His Holy Spirit and freed from the bondage of any lies that have held you captive.

As my pastor always prays before he preaches, may we leave differently than we came in.

Chapter 1:

A DEEP ACHE

It began as a subtle nagging in my heart, like the elusive pain when a tooth starts having problems. This pain creeps in with a dull ache. You know it's there, but it's easy to push the pain aside and ignore it because it doesn't feel like a big deal at the moment. Yet, all the while, there is a bigger problem brewing deep down underneath the surface.

I felt something stirring within me, like a storm brewing in the distance, but it was easy to push aside those feelings in the busyness of life.

At that point in life, my husband and I had been married for a few years and had two young boys at home who needed my dedicated attention and kept me busy. We spent most of our time going to church activities throughout the week and on the weekends, and we didn't have many other relationships outside of church and family.

Motherhood was lonely at times. I tried going to local groups for moms, but breaking into other friendship groups was difficult. I tried connecting with moms at my kids' schools, but making friendships there wasn't easy either. I tried getting the kids together with their school friends outside of school, but I came up against a lot of resistance. All this made me feel like I was doing the mom thing alone most of the time, and I felt discouraged and defeated because my attempts to create friendships for me or my children weren't working out.

For most of our earlier married years, my husband and I attended the church I grew up in. I had stepped away from this church during my prodigal years but returned to it later. We were married and dedicated our children there, so there were emotional attachments to the church.

The church went through a massive split while we were attending there as a family. This division was messy, hurtful, and ungodly on so many levels. At least half the congregation left; some went to other churches, and others started a home church, where we began to attend.

The things I watched during this split shook my heart and made me ask God some questions. Growing up there, I knew several of the people involved in the situation, and now I began seeing these people and situations through an adult lens instead of a child's. That was devastating to me.

The home church we started attending was similar to the original church in some ways and quite different in others. It had a warm, personal atmosphere that was a refreshing change from the trappings of a regimented worship style I had experienced as a young person.

Still, I felt that I was missing something.

I continued reading the Bible, praying, and doing all the other things on my spiritual checklist and mental Rolodex cards. We went to church on Saturdays and to prayer night once a week. I was involved in the women's ministry whenever possible; I dressed modestly on our tight budget and did my best to look like a good Christian woman, wife, and mother. I wore my masks well and was an expert at shoving my feelings so far down beneath the surface that no one could see them.

* * *

Religion calls us to put on masks to make things look better than they are in real life. We smile and laugh while we are breaking inside. We people-please while we deny ourselves the freedom to be who God created us to be with the gifts, needs, and purposes He has placed within us. We put on the act like we have it all together, while the reality is we are falling apart.

This is what I had learned to do from a young age. I learned to ignore the things I struggled with and the things that hurt me. After all, what would people say if they knew the depths of the brokenness inside me?

Isn't that the lie the enemy whispers to all of us?

In my head, I knew God loved and forgave me, but I wasn't able to let this head knowledge trickle down into the roots of my heart and become real. I was still stuck in a life of religion.

I don't know your story, and even though our stories may have different details, I imagine our feelings could be the same. Do you recognize the ache I have been talking about? Have you been trying to ignore it?

Have you learned to shove those feelings down deep inside or put on the mask while you struggle to keep hanging on without giving others a glimpse of your heart? Have you been going through the motions but continue to feel empty?

I would challenge you to pause and ask God to show you if you've been hiding. He doesn't want you living that way. He is faithful to bring it all to the surface so we can deal with it and move forward in a relationship with Him. That is precisely what He did for me.

A relationship with Jesus invites us to come as we are and lay these burdens, hurts, and anxieties at His feet. He asks us to be still and know Him and to allow Him to come into those hurt places and bring healing and freedom.

The pain from the subtle ache inside me became more noticeable. I couldn't walk away anymore and ignore it as I had been doing. But I was bewildered about what it meant.

One day, it all came to a head. The ache was throbbing like an infected tooth. I could no longer ignore it or console myself with temporary comfort. There was a hole in my heart that nothing could fill. I couldn't fill it with my spiritual to-do list, my ceaseless striving, or hiding behind my mask of false security.

I knew I couldn't keep living this way. I could feel myself dying inside, and something had to change.

After getting ready for church one morning, I sat my boys at the kitchen table with their breakfast. Attempting not to bring any attention to myself, I quickly slipped away into the bathroom, quietly closing the door behind me. I slumped down onto the side of the cold porcelain tub and started to weep.

The tears broke through like a dam, bursting and overflowing onto my face and down my shirt. All I had been holding in for years just poured out. I cried out to God that morning in the bathroom, seeking to understand. I was rawer and more honest with God than I ever had dared to be before. "There has to be more to this Christian life than this vicious cycle I've been living in," I sobbed. "Please let there be more because I don't want to live this way anymore."

I sat in God's presence for what felt like hours until I heard one of my sons call for me. His voice brought me back to reality, and I remembered that I needed to finish getting them ready for church.

That day was the beginning of an enduring journey for me. I had lived a religiously legalistic Christian life for a long time and was like a computer that was spiritually programmed to live a certain way. My life had become practically robotic without much thought or feeling. Church was not much different, but now God was about to reprogram me and renew my mind.

Did you grow up in the church? Or have you been a Christian for a long time, yet you sense something is missing? Do you know there is more to life, but you can't seem to figure out what it is? Have you done all you know to do, yet it never seems to be enough, and you feel as empty as you did before?

As we walk through this reprogramming process together, I pray God meets you where you are, just like He did for me. I pray He opens your eyes and heart to see and know the abundant life He has called us to live.

Jesus came to set the captives free!

Recently, I was reading in Acts 9 about Saul's conversion on the Damascus Road. When I read it, the conversation came to life a little differently for me than it had in the past.

Saul believed he was living for God. He followed the laws and the rules as a Jewish scholar and a Roman citizen. Saul was a faithful Pharisee, and he was proud of it. He knew Scripture, and his heart was sincere. He genuinely believed he was doing what was right by persecuting Christians.

He saw Christianity as a threat to Judaism until the day he met Jesus on the Damascus Road. Saul was reprogrammed, too. God renewed his mind and transformed His heart (see Acts 9:10).

Meeting Jesus changed Saul's life forever, the same way it changed mine and the same way it will change yours if you willingly reach out your hand to grab His.

Just like with me, Jesus is reaching His hand out to you. He wants to walk with you in this life. He wants to renew your mind and transform your heart, which is what a relationship with Jesus does.

Will you allow Him to take your hand, walk with you, and break down all the walls that religion has built up? Let's do this together!

Chapter 2:

TAKE ME IN YOUR ARMS: FROM JUDGE TO FATHER

"Don't do this and don't do that" was everyday talk in the church and at home when I was young, and the emotion behind the words escalated when I did anything in the "don't" section. My mistakes created anger and disappointment in myself and others. I developed the mindset that to be worthy enough for my parents, church family, other people, and God, I had to do all the right things all the time. For a long time, I didn't realize how much these earthly physical experiences affected my relationship with God and how I perceived Him as my heavenly Father.

The "do" category usually included people's personal expectations, opinions, rules, and regulations that other people interpreted from the Bible.

Growing up, praises and acknowledgment of my obedience, victories, or successes seemed scarce, yet when I failed or messed up, someone was right there to point it out, criticize, or reprimand me.

My heart wanted to do things right and well, but despite how much I tried, I couldn't do everything everyone around me, including myself, wanted or expected, and the things I did wrong were the ones talked about, pointed out, and almost impossible to live down. The enemy took this and ran with it, building on the lies sitting idle in my mind. The disappointed faces and words of loved ones affirmed the lies the enemy continued to whisper to me and confirmed the condemnation and shame in my heart.

In the introduction of this book, I shared about my season of walking away from God. Through that experience, I learned how much God genuinely loved me. I noticed when everyone else walked away, He stayed, and when everyone around me thought my life was over and beyond repair, God saw it as just the beginning.

As I began to come back to my relationship with Jesus after living in religion for so long, I found myself trying to make up for my mistakes by attempting to "do" all the right things and be the perfect wife, mom, friend, and Christian woman I thought I was supposed to be. My biggest fear was that if I disappointed Him, He wouldn't be pleased with me anymore or take away the forgiveness I had already received.

In my mind, I held a visual of a judge slamming down the gavel and shouting "guilty!" ready to sentence me.

When "don't" is the main word used to teach, defeat is mainly what people feel and live.

When we see others, do we only point out what we see is wrong, or do we see the things they do right, too? Do we compliment someone when we see they have been thoughtful or loving to someone else or to us? Do we encourage that husband or wife when we see them loving their spouse well? Do we build up that young mom when we see she is doing her best with her children? Do we encourage that person we see being obedient to God when it is really hard for them to do?

I don't remember many times throughout my life when people encouraged and cheered me on when I did something right or when I was thoughtful or helpful. During that same time, it's hard for me to recall being urged to move in the right direction or being recognized for making a good choice or doing something well. This taught me that even in the imperfection of a task, we need to see the genuine desire of a person's heart to do it well and the effort they are putting in. Even though this was the way I wanted to live, it took a while to break out of that religious cycle of doing the same thing to others.

One day, I yelled at my young son out of frustration and probably made him feel the same way I had always felt—like a failure in every area of life. I reflected on that moment when God whispered those words to my hurting and defeated heart: "You keep trying to earn and receive what has already been given to you." He loved me because I was His. I was forgiven when I repented, and I didn't have to keep trying to make up for anything or attempt to earn His love and forgiveness. It was already mine.

God's message was completely different from what I had received from others, even those in the church and the body of Christ. He loved me. He forgave me and wanted to help me become the wife, mom, friend, and Christian woman He created me to be because that is His heart.

God wasn't waiting for me to make a mistake so He could point it out and shake his finger at me to keep me in the cycle of condemnation and shame I had lived in for years. He wanted me to live in victory and freedom, secure in His love for me. God also wanted to teach me. He wanted to show me how to live this life, not just tell me what not to do.

That is the beautiful thing about our heavenly Father. He sees us in those places where we are stuck and striving. He knows our hearts' motivation and desire to do things well. He doesn't just leave us there, keeping us in shame and condemnation with His words and actions.

He comes alongside us, reaching His hand down to us to lift us up. He shows us where we are wrong, convicts our hearts, grabs our hands, and shows us the way to go. He is there to ask questions and to seek Him out when we don't know where to go or what to do. He is there when we don't do something well or strive too hard to do what we think is expected of us. He walks with us and guides us with His Holy Spirit, our helper.

This is a vastly different view of God than many of us have been taught about or experienced.

After yelling at my son, I hugged him and told him I was sorry. I repented and asked God to help me teach my son differently, to know how to come alongside him and speak a different message than I had received as a child. I wanted to teach him, not just with the "don'ts" but also by praising him when he listened and obeyed, when he was kind to his brother, or in those moments when he was helpful to me. I wanted to be a mom who saw the good things, too, not just the mistakes and the moments of rebellion.

My heart began softening that day; it was more encouraged and hopeful than it had been in a long time. My view of God being an angry judge ready to condemn, put me down, and impose a harsh sentence on me began to change.

Instead, I began seeing Him as my heavenly Father who loved and wanted me and who was reaching out His hand, inviting me to walk with Him. He offered open arms so He could embrace, love, comfort, and show me the right way to go. When I felt like a complete failure, He invited me to give Him my tears, frustrations, and pain.

I know that many of us have had earthly family situations that have not always reflected the true heart of our heavenly Father. These experiences cause us to question whether it's safe to mess up or be imperfect. It causes us to keep God at arm's length when He wants us in His arms. He wants to love us, comfort us, and keep us safe. He wants to walk us through those struggles.

One thing I love about God is that He gives us earthly experiences that show us the things He is teaching us, so we have a picture of it right in front of us.

One of my favorite moments at a wedding is the father and daughter dance. I hear the announcement and wait in anticipation. A song begins to play, always something unique that represents their relationship, and then the father and daughter walk toward the dance floor. The father reaches out his hand to his daughter, inviting her to join him. She takes it, and he gently draws her near him, and they dance. He leads, and they move together in unity. Some moments are spent talking, but in other moments, they smile at one another with a familiar look, and you know their thoughts are shared in that moment. At other times, I simply see the daughter's head resting on her father's shoulder as they glide along the dance floor together. You can sense the love and beauty of that relationship, which is known to everyone in the room.

I smile, and tears flow down as I think about this dance because it's a beautiful picture for us.

Our heavenly Father knows life has been hard for us sometimes. He knows people have represented Him wrongly and unfairly to us, but He wants to give us what we have always been afraid to receive. He wants to give His love, forgiveness, and a place of belonging. We don't have to be afraid. We can let go and allow Him to renew our mindset and reprogram our idea of who He is and who He is to us.

He wants to heal those wounded places and enable us to trust Him.

He wants to draw us close and to lead us.

His arm is out, and His hand is ready for you. Will you allow Him to take you in His arms and love you as your heavenly Father?

Chapter 3:

DANCING FOR AN AUDIENCE OF ONE

One day, I was out and about on the town. My eyes were drawn toward a young girl sitting with her family. While I observed their time together, the sweet young girl jumped down from her seat, and I watched as she began dancing around. Her beautiful blue eyes rested on her father. I saw her heart longing to impress this important man in her life. At that moment, I could tell his affection, focus, and pleasure were all that mattered to her.

As she danced for him, a big smile broke out on his face. He beamed with pride and joy as he lovingly watched his daughter—from the moment she stood up to the moment she took a bow. Then he met her with arms wide open. The hug he gave her and the words he spoke expressed how pleased he was with her.

This delightful, heartfelt moment triggered a place deep within me. My mind raced back through memories of moments when I have been like that little girl, desiring to be noticed and appreciated and longing to feel special and loved. Often, I didn't receive the same response the young girl received. Instead, I received words that critiqued who I was and expressed a desire for me to be more like someone else. Who I was didn't seem good enough to please those around me. I felt like more of a disappointment than a source of pride.

This constant feeling of disappointment and not measuring up to who I should be continued to follow me like a shadow into my relationship with God. Even after I returned from my prodigal years, I found myself constantly jumping off my seat, always performing and begging to hear that my heavenly Father was pleased with me.

This residual mess inside my heart left me feeling as though I were never good enough. I had to perform and focus on doing just the right things to keep my heavenly Father's attention. I found myself spiraling into a life of bondage and constantly feeling like it was what I did or didn't do that defined my worth. This translated into a people-pleasing lifestyle and a constant battle with measuring up.

BREAKING THE CHAINS

We have an enemy who wants us to question God and His love for us. We see this in Genesis 3. The serpent asks Eve questions, making her doubt God's intentions and His love and care for her. Some of us were often told that we were disappointments, or we've had our failures called out in front of others so often that there is a severe fear of failure. We've been conditioned to expect rejection when we disappoint or fail to perform. This leads to feeling like we are constantly failing or disappointing God, leading to the hamster wheel of striving to be seen, loved, and known.

But the chains fall off when we receive God's truth: we are loved for who we are, right where we are. He has given us everything we need to go forward in victory and freedom. Religion says we must earn grace and acceptance. A relationship with Jesus says He has already earned it for us. It is finished. Religion requires perfection. A relationship with Jesus says to live out of His perfection.

This is freedom. Learning how to live out of His perfection instead of our own attempted perfection gives us the freedom to make mistakes, fail, and learn. Mistakes will always be here on this side of Heaven, but there is repentance, healing, freedom, and victory in Jesus. When God looks at us, He sees Jesus. When we live in Jesus, we abide in Him.

John 15:4–8 says:

> Abide in Me, and I in you. As the branch cannot bear fruit of itself unless it abides in the vine, neither can you unless you abide in Me. I am the vine; you are the branches; he who abides in Me and I in him, he bears much fruit, for apart from Me you can do nothing. If anyone does not abide in Me, he is thrown away as a branch and dries up; and they gather them, and cast them into the fire, and they are burned. If you abide in Me, and My words abide in you, ask whatever you wish, and it will be done

> for you. My Father is glorified by this, that you bear much fruit, and so prove to be My disciples.

For me, as I abide in Jesus, it means going to His Word, talking to Him in prayer, or simply going somewhere quiet and peaceful and sitting in God's presence silently, listening for His still, small voice in this loud and crazy world. Sometimes, it means drawing close to Him when everything in me feels like pulling away because I am angry, frustrated, or hurt.

When we do this, we remember who He is and who He is to us personally. We find freedom from the condemnation and shame that threaten to take over our hearts and minds, causing us to live in that religious place.

BREAKING THE CYCLE

Unfortunately, sometimes, we as Christians can keep each other in bondage by holding each other to standards only Jesus can meet. We hold ourselves and others to these standards, which keep us stuck inside the confines of religion instead of fully transitioning to a relationship with Jesus.

How do we break this cycle?

How do we spur one another on toward a life of relationship with Jesus?

First, we must receive God's genuine love for us. We need to remember Romans 5:6–8: "For while we were still helpless, at the right time Christ died for the ungodly. For one will hardly die for a righteous man, though perhaps for the good man someone would dare even to die. But God demonstrates His own love toward us, in that while we were yet sinners, Christ died for us."

God loved us so much, he had Jesus die for us—not when we were perfect and all put together, but when we were sinners. He rose from the dead and gave us a way back to that relationship with the Father. He loved us because we are His. He loved us before we got put back together. He saw who we could be in Jesus.

Second, we accept Jesus as our Savior. Jesus came to free us from the bondage of religion. We see this in the life of Paul.

Paul was born into a Hebrew family and was part of the Tribe of Benjamin. He was fluent in Old Testament Scripture and a devout Jew, extremely devoted to God's law. He was also a Pharisee (see Acts 23:6; Philippians 3:4–6). *Merriam-Webster* defines Pharisee as "a member of a Jewish sect of the intertestamental period noted for strict observance of rites and ceremonies of the written law and for insistence on the validity of their own oral traditions concerning the law and a person who is marked by hypocritical censorious self-righteousness."[1]

Not only was Paul a Pharisee, he was a *zealous* Pharisee. He believed that the new believers were blasphemous and heretical. He believed they were dishonoring God and was doing all he could to bring justice to them, even to the point of killing them (see Philippians 3:4–6; Acts 8:1–3; Acts 9:1–2). Then, one day, on the Damascus Road, he met Jesus. His eyes were opened to who Jesus truly is, and God began preparing him for what he had called him to do. He began to preach about Jesus and the Gospel message instead of putting people to death or in prison (see Acts 9:3–31). He led them into a relationship with Jesus and brought them to where they could find freedom.

At first, Paul believed he was doing what was right. He had grown up knowing the Jewish faith and following the law. Paul had been taught how to live a life of religion, and he was defending it to the death. As he lived out that life of religion, he put people to death, sent them to prison, and condemned them with his words. He was a bully.

When we live a life of religion, we, too, can become bullies with our words and our actions.

When Paul met Jesus, his life and heart changed. He became the one God chose to send the Gospel message to the Gentiles. Paul learned that what He had been doing for God really wasn't what God wanted.

QUESTIONS TO THINK ABOUT

How many things do we do just because we were raised or taught to do them?

How often have we been more concerned about people's behavior or ensuring they are following the law than about the condition of their hearts?

How many times have we gossiped about, condemned, or put down others because they aren't doing what we think they should be doing?

Just like Paul, we have put people in prison mentally, emotionally, and spiritually because of these things. We have helped the enemy by telling people what they do or don't do defines them. Instead, we should remind them and ourselves that a relationship with Jesus defines who we are and changes us from the inside out. Believing otherwise causes us to jump off our seats and start performing all the time.

NO MORE PERFORMING

As I watched the interaction between the father and the daughter that day, I saw the father's smile and look of love on his face the whole time he was with his daughter. It was there before the performance, and it was there after the performance. His love for her was evident. His open arms and embrace weren't simply for the performance but because she was his.

Our heavenly Father is smiling; He looks at us with love and doesn't need a performance from us. He just needs us. He has unique things planned for us to do, and He will share those things with us as we live in a relationship with Jesus.

No matter what you have been taught, how you have been raised, or what others have said to you, you only dance for an audience of one: The One who created you, the One who designed you to be who you are, and the One who has planned your life with good things to do. His arms are wide open, inviting you in to be loved and known by Him. He is smiling and full of joy that you are His. He loves you more than anything, and His embrace and approval are all you need.

Chapter 4:

THE LOVE LETTER OF GOD'S WORD

Dating in the 1990s was nothing like it is now. People didn't send emails or texts, and we didn't use smartphones or social media. All we had were regular house phones with short or long cords (if we were lucky) and handwritten letters.

When my husband, Duane, and I began dating, he lived in South Carolina, and I lived in Rhode Island. At that time, there were significant charges for long distance calling, so between the cost of phone calls and the challenge of understanding conversation on the phone due to my severe hearing loss, our main form of communication was writing letters. We wrote letters to get to know each other and build our relationship.

Unlike emails, texting, and social media, letters took days or weeks to get to the other person. I would calculate how long it took for a letter to get to my husband, allowing one day's time for him to write back and mail the letter and another few days for it to travel by post to me. If he wrote me back immediately, a letter would take about a week to arrive. In between life activities, I often glanced out the window, hoping to catch a peek of the mailman coming so I could snatch the letter up as soon as possible. I couldn't wait to read what Duane had written.

When his letter finally arrived, I would sneak away somewhere private to rip open the envelope like a gift on Christmas morning. I soaked up every written word like a sponge, melting inside as I read the words on the page written specifically for me.

THE BIBLE: GOD'S LOVE LETTER TO US

Have you ever thought about how God's Word was written specifically for each of us? It's the most amazing personal love letter of all.

Growing up in the church, I felt like the Bible was a book we saw on the shelf until it was time for church, Bible study, or prayer meeting; then it was pulled down and the dust carefully wiped away. There was a desire to hide any perceived or real lack of use because we needed to look the part of a Christian.

As a young person, I watched people carry Bibles into the church, and some were even prettied up with crochet or leather covers on them. I'm not saying there's anything wrong with this, but often there seemed to be a "look at me" attitude and a sense of arrogance as people paraded their Bibles, much like the Pharisees in Matthew 6:5: "When you pray you are not to be like the hypocrites; for they love to stand and pray in the synagogues and on the street corners so that they may be seen by men. Truly, I say to you, they have their reward in full."

Religion is good at making things appear much prettier or better than they really are in real life, and I felt like the Bible was more about appearance and playing the part of the "good Christian."

Another practice that focused on appearances was the massive emphasis on memorizing Scripture. Now, don't get me wrong; memorizing Scripture is an important practice. However, when memorizing and reciting God's Word in front of others becomes more important than knowing the One who wrote it, then memorization isn't fruitful.

For me, memorizing Scripture was difficult. I struggled to keep the words seared in my mind, so I constantly felt like a failure in that department. In the church, memorization was a huge focal point and felt like an identity marker. If you did it well, you got a gold star and lots of applause, which identified you as a five-star Christian. If you didn't do it well, there was no gold star or applause for you, just disappointment from those around you and taunting words and looks from those who could memorize verses easily and quickly. Again, I would come away after reading God's Word feeling empty, alone, and defeated.

Even Bible studies seemed shallow. We would read a passage and answer questions, but the answers simply repeated what we just read. There wasn't much depth to the questions, and the conversations around the study were surface level. Discussions were informational, not relational, and they didn't center around building a relationship with Jesus. Few people shared any real personal experiences.

As a younger believer, I would look down at the pages of my Bible, feeling as if I was reading about a distant God. The more I read, the more distant I felt. I wondered how the One who wrote these words could really love or desire me. The condemnation and shame caused me to want to read the Bible less and not more. Unlike with my husband's letters, I didn't have a personal connection with the author of this letter.

What was the cause of this disconnect?

CONNECTING WITH THE AUTHOR

With Duane, I got to know him more as a person from his letters, and his words had meaning to me. The intention of his letters was to get to know me better and share himself with me to help me know him better.

God's Word had been presented to me more as a rule book or just a storybook about someone instead of the love letter God intended for it to be. Religion says God's Word is a ruler to measure how good you are (as well as other people). A relationship with Jesus says: This is God's love letter to you, to know His love for you, and for you to get to know His heart.

At the beginning of my relationship with Jesus, I desired to be in the Word. That goal sat at the top of my spiritual checklist daily and was written on my mental Rolodex cards. I would read Scripture, smile, and close the Bible feeling accomplished in doing what I was supposed to do that day.

I don't remember feeling as though I knew God better at all. It was more about facts, learning about a person in the Bible, or just being able to tell people I was in the Word that day. God still seemed so distant to me, and I couldn't understand why.

Do you ever feel this way after being in God's Word?

What is it that causes the disconnect for you?

For me, there were several things I discovered about myself. God's Word had become like lemon juice in a wound for me. I was repentant and fully remorseful for the things I had done in the past and felt equally sorry for my wrong words, attitudes, and actions in the present. But if we go to God's Word legalistically and religiously without the heart of God, we end up focusing more on the dos and don'ts. Reading God's Word then becomes more about modifying our behavior than changing our hearts. This was how the Pharisees were behaving when Christ called them out, saying, "But woe to you, scribes and Pharisees, hypocrites!" (see Matthew 23:13–29). This is how I felt I needed to be. I put on a show for the outside without knowing who I needed to become on the inside.

If we don't understand what God did for us through Jesus, we will continually feel condemned and shamed after reading God's Word. All we'll hear is what we are doing wrong instead of who God says we are in Him and what He wants for us. That message doesn't create an environment where we want to know God more. Since I heard this message so much as a child, I wanted to avoid putting myself in places to be torn down as an adult. Who wants to do that? The enemy used this lie to keep me from connecting with Jesus the way He wanted to connect with me in His Word.

Growing up in religion in the church brought about another struggle for me. We weren't really taught how to study

God's Word to know who He is and to know and understand what He is saying to us there. We rarely discussed the Holy Spirit except when He showed up for Jesus's baptism. I didn't know how to dig deeper into God's Word. I didn't know I could simply ask the Holy Spirit to help me understand and discern what God was saying in His Word and to me personally:

> I will ask the Father, and He will give you another Helper, that He may be with you forever; that is the Spirit of truth, whom the world cannot receive because it does not see Him or know Him, but you know Him because He abides with you and will be in you. (John 14:16)

> But when He, the Spirit of truth, comes, He will guide you into all the truth; for He will not speak on His own initiative, but whatever He hears, He will speak; and He will disclose to you what is to come. He will glorify Me, for He will take of Mine and will disclose it to you. All things that the Father has are Mine; therefore I said that He takes of Mine and will disclose it to you. (John 16:13)

THE AUTHOR WANTS US TO KNOW HIM!

God loved us so much that when Jesus went to Heaven to be with the Father, the Holy Spirit came to live in us to be our helper. He never leaves us alone. We have been given the Holy Spirit to help us know and discern all God wants to share with us.

How amazing is it that God loves us so much that He wants us to know His heart, the truth, and His secrets? Like a friend, He wants to spend time with us, and He wants us to know Him. He doesn't want to be a distant and disconnected God. The Holy Spirit is proof of this.

God's Word doesn't need to be overwhelming. We have a helper. Before you open the Bible, take a moment and ask the Holy Spirit to guide you into all truth as you read the words on those pages. Then ask the Holy Spirit to reveal all God has to say to you and to help you know God's heart. Watch and see how it makes a difference.

Religion makes God's Word seem unapproachable and hard to understand. A relationship with Jesus gives us the boldness to approach His Word without fear, knowing God will make Himself known to us.

Do you see God's Word as a book of stories or a rule book? Are you like me in that this is how you were taught to look at the Bible?

When my husband and I wrote to one another, we asked each other questions. We sought to know and understand the person our hearts were being drawn toward. We began to open up and share more, going into a deeper understanding of one another. This is what God's Word is to us: a love letter. We can come with our questions, and He reveals Himself one truth at a time as we seek Him.

Some of us come from a place where we have never even seen a Bible for different reasons; others have been taught that someone else must dictate the Bible to them, but that isn't the truth. Maybe we've learned the Scriptures and have many of them memorized in our heads, yet none of it lies in our hearts. Others of us have dabbled in the Word, reading the words but not knowing anything about the one who writes them, so they feel impersonal and harsh.

The process of God renewing my mind in this area has taken some time. It started when I began to see God as a Father who loves me and desires a relationship with me. With those truths fresh in my mind, I began taking steps, one Scripture and one prayer at a time, asking the Holy Spirit to reveal the truth to me, and journaling. I bought a study Bible, a Bible dictionary, and I began using Bible study tools. I joined Bible studies and small groups to study God's Word with others who wanted to know God more personally.

As I took these steps with a sincere heart to know Him, seeking Him along the way, He began to show me His heart and His Word, bringing it to life for me:

"For the word of God is living and active and sharper than any two-edged sword, and piercing as far as the division of soul and spirit, of both joints and marrow, and able to judge the thoughts and intentions of the heart. And there is no creature hidden from His sight, but all things are open and laid bare to the eyes of Him with whom we have to do" (Heb. 4:12–13).

THE POWER OF GOD'S WORD

God's Word has become alive to me. Each time I go to it, even if I'm reading a Scripture I've seen a thousand times, He brings it to life to me for exactly where I am that day. He uses it to speak to me personally. His Word also reveals my heart: where I need to repent, where I need to grow, and where I need to rest. He shows me my attitudes, my hurts, and when I slip back into performance mode or those people-pleasing cycles. In the Bible, I see God's heart as He reminds me who He is, who I am to Him, and His promises to me in this crazy, weary, and sometimes painful life.

How could seeing your Bible as God's personal love letter to you change your approach to His Word and your willingness to go back to it continually?

I pray that as you grab your Bible off your shelf this week, you won't be ashamed of the dust or the time that has passed since you looked at it the last time. Instead, just like on the days I received those letters from my husband, I pray you would run to a quiet and private place, rip open that Bible, and soak up every word. Ask questions and ask the Holy Spirit to lead you into the truth of who God is and who you are to Him. Ask Him to reveal His heart to you and get to know the One who knows you better than anyone, the One who loves you more than anyone ever will.

Watch that beautiful relationship blossom into something you never imagined that will bless your heart forever.

Chapter 5:

PRAYER: TRANSFORMATION FROM ACQUAINTANCE TO FRIEND

When we walked into Christian Hill Community Church for the first time in fall 2007, I had just had a second cochlear implant surgery less than a year before. I was adjusting to listening with two implanted ears. We had come out of a small church experience, so I was used to being in a building with far fewer people, all of whom were familiar to me.

We had been praying about where God wanted us to be as far as a local church. He provided an opportunity for my husband to get a job at Christian Hill Community Church as a facilities manager. When he took the job, we committed to be there for a year to see if God affirmed this as our home church. Seventeen years later, we are still there, deeply involved and invested.

Christian Hill Community Church is not a small church. In fact, it's quite the opposite. Around 600 to 650 people attend between the two services every Sunday. Needless to say, it was a little overwhelming and a huge adjustment for us because we came from a small church. Between my hearing loss and my not having many experiences with friendships and social situations, I struggled with being socially awkward. When my husband had to work somewhere in the building, my two boys and I sat in the seats at Christian Hill without him. I was an anxious mess.

At first, I thought that sitting alone was bad, but then Pastor Dave told us to greet someone next to us and say hello. At this point, I knew no one. I felt like a complete stranger in that place, and I was very intimidated. So I quickly said hi, smiled, and then sat down and prayed so I wouldn't seem rude.

When I was introduced to people, I was typically addressed as "Duane's wife." For a while, it felt like I hid behind that identity. I would smile, trying to muster up conversation and at least make some acquaintances. Deep down, though, my heart longed for real friendship and relationships.

At my last church, people saw each other at church, but we rarely experienced friendships that went deeper than that, where we really knew each other. Friendships didn't extend beyond the time at church together, so people felt more like acquaintances than friends. I believe this created part of the deep ache I talked about back in chapter 1: a longing for more than just casual relationships and a longing for authentic, meaningful, and deep relationships with God and other people.

GOING DEEPER

As I take time to look back to where I started in my prayer journey, I can see that this awkward time was where a deeper relationship with God began for me. I was that anxious young woman, glancing over and quickly saying hi, before I sat down in my seat. I didn't know God. He was an acquaintance to me. I knew some things about Him but didn't even know who I was talking to, how to talk to Him, or what to talk to Him about. He intimidated me because He was God, and I was a very imperfect young wife, mom, and person.

Up until this point, most of my prayer experience, outside saying grace before a meal, was repeating a prayer that someone else wrote in a book or at the end of a devotional. Prayer equated to my asking for something, or someone praying to end the time together in class or at an activity. My prayer life changed when I began to pray Scripture. I had heard this was a good way to start to pray, so that is what I did.

This experience reminded me of my children when they were learning to talk. They mimicked us and repeated the things we said. They didn't know what the words meant, but they knew they were saying our words back to us.

I didn't know or understand everything I was praying at times, but other times, I was repeating God's words back to Him, which other people said was a powerful thing. As a young mom and a wife, I loved the books by Stormie Omartian. I read *The Power of a Praying Wife* and *The Power of a Praying Parent.* I would read the books and pray, inserting my name, my husband's name, or my children's. I have since moved on to *The Power of Praying for Your Adult Children.*

These are wonderful tools and have been helpful for me in my prayer journey, but I sometimes felt my prayers were a little lifeless, and I experienced a deep aching inside, like there was something more to prayer that I was missing.

When I went to prayer meetings, I battled a religious mindset. I heard some people pray so elegantly, and all I could do was sit there and try to think of how I could pray. I didn't want to sound too simple or accidentally say something that sounded unintelligible. These thoughts crowded my mind while, at the same time, I tried to hear and understand what was being said so I could pop into the group to pray. Needless to say, I was not connecting with the Lord much.

I felt like how I presented my prayers out loud defined me as a Christian. When words flowed well out of my mouth, I walked away feeling more like I did a great job that night or I was a little more holy. I didn't realize the Holy Spirit was praying with me because I was too focused on praying for performance. I spent more time praying for prayer requests and what I needed or thought someone else needed than praising the One I was praying to or thanking Him for who He is, what He had done for me, and what He was still doing for me.

Prayer meetings were more about the long list of prayer needs and not as much about praise. There were some praises here or there, but the focus was on the prayer list that came out after talking for a half hour to forty-five minutes or, if in a woman's group, the prayer requests easily turned into a gossip session. I also noticed that people presented prayer requests about other people or church situations. People weren't transparent in asking for prayer for themselves. But the truth is that when we are transparent, we become vulnerable. When we're concerned about appearances and how we look, we can't be transparent and vulnerable. When we pray out of a religious mindset, the focus is on us.

GOD TEACHES US AS WE PRACTICE

As God began showing me those things, I began practicing gratitude more. I would say at least one thing I was thankful for, and I used the book of Psalms to verbally praise Him. I practiced being intentional in showing praise and gratitude for who He is, and I took time to acknowledge Him.

I also spent more time in God's Word to try and understand more of who He is so I could praise Him from a more genuine place. Slowly, He was becoming more than an acquaintance.

One day, I was cleaning while the boys were at school, and my cochlear implants were off for a break. Listening to the vacuum cleaner is not a happy sound for me, so I love cleaning with my "ears" off. As I moved through the house, vacuuming, mopping, and cleaning toilets, I realized I had been praying in my mind and spirit. The Holy Spirit had been putting some things on my heart. There were people I had thought of and prayed about. I had been thinking about a decision we needed to make, and I had some doubts about it. I wrestled with fear and anxiety in different areas of my life, and I talked to God about all these topics and more. All while I was cleaning the house!

God showed me that while I was cleaning and doing other things, I wasn't talking. In those moments, I was just being with God. He was with me as I was cleaning. I wasn't talking, and I didn't have all the distracting life sounds around me like I usually did, so He was able to speak more to me, and it became more of a casual conversation and quality time with Him.

This was the beginning of my really learning to hear Him and discerning the Holy Spirit's nudges, prodding, and God's voice. I don't think we really understand the importance of being in prayer. Religion makes it all about what we are supposed to do, say, and act like while we are in prayer.

A DEEPER RELATIONSHIP WITH JESUS LEADS TO DEEPER RELATIONSHIPS WITH OTHERS

Relationship with Jesus is more about *being* with Him and *knowing* Him.

It wasn't until I began spending time with those new people God had put in my life at church that relationships started building. It took time serving together and sharing coffee together; those were the times I talked, listened, and learned about who they were as the people God created. One of my favorite verses in the Bible is Psalm 46:10: "Cease striving and know that I am God; I will be exalted among the nations, I will be exalted in the earth."

Religion calls us to strive. Relationship with Jesus calls us to stop striving and be still. Our culture constantly demands our time and mental and emotional space, and this life has numerous responsibilities. To sit and cease striving requires intentionality. Relationships require intentionality.

If I never take time to be with my husband, my children, or these new people in my life, how will any of those relationships grow or thrive? In any relationship where no one is putting the time in or when the relationship becomes one-sided, the intentional person gets weary, and the relationship suffers or dies off.

When we cease striving to be still with God, we get to know Him better and in a deeper way. We don't just talk, we listen. In the stillness, we experience His presence personally, and we connect with our heavenly Father in a way we can't when we are running around like crazy, our minds on everything around us but Him.

I was amazed as I spent time cleaning with my cochlear implants off. Without them on, I don't hear any sound, so I am literally in my own little world. I realized I was hearing God clearer when all the world's sounds were literally shut off. I am in complete dead silence. A silence the hearing world can't understand.

This truth made me weep for a moment. Not sad tears but happy tears. My hearing loss wasn't able to keep me from having a full and close relationship with God. In fact, it has really drawn me closer to Him.

In my process of building relationships with new people at church, my hearing loss does affect things. I may miss things and misunderstand things easily. It is more work for the other person to take time to be intentionally looking at me and pronouncing things well. When I am struggling to understand or dealing with sensory overload, my facial expressions can come across the wrong way. It makes getting to know me harder sometimes because there is so much to try to explain to someone who hasn't been through the hearing loss and deafness experience.

But with God, He created me; He knows me. He breaks through all the barriers. I still misunderstand Him sometimes, but He never misunderstands me. The more I learn to be in prayer, the more the words flow naturally, and the time spent together grows our relationship deeper.

Over time, I have learned His voice. I know when He is tugging on my heart and when He is redirecting me. I have learned to discern between conviction from Him and condemnation from the enemy. God becomes my best friend and the One I run to first (most of the time, anyway).

We have been at Christian Hill for seventeen years, and seeing how God has grown our relationships there is amazing. God has answered my prayer for friends. He went beyond that and gave us family there. He's used this place to get me out of my comfort zone, and now I go up to new people and say hi without any reservations whatsoever! My husband and I now joke about how many people now know him as "Desiree's husband"!

Religion keeps us timid and insecure when we pray because we see God as an acquaintance instead of going deeper in our relationship with Him. It makes prayer all about us and nothing about God. We get stuck in life because we continue to stay dependent on ourselves, and we run to everything and everyone else but the One who has the answers for everything in this life. Religion keeps us striving.

A relationship with Jesus teaches us how to be still and know the One who knows and loves us more than anyone on earth. He is the One who knows every step we need to take and has every answer we need—the One who is there every moment of every day and desires that we reach out to Him.

If God has only been an acquaintance to you, take the small steps toward getting to know Him. Spend time being still and encountering Him in a new way. God wants to be your Father and your friend. Will you let Him?

Chapter 6:

LEARNING WHO I AM THROUGH THE EYES OF JESUS

Shortly after my cochlear implant surgeries and learning to hear with them, I realized the world is extremely loud and noisy. There are constant sounds and voices around us all the time. This was surprising and overwhelming for me as a person who was hard of hearing and someone who had lost almost *all* her hearing. I wondered how hearing people could live in this eternal noise without the ability to take a break and shut it off. There were moments when the sensory overload was unbearable.

In a similar way, life is always noisy. There are voices all around us, speaking and communicating things to our hearts and minds that affect us—sometimes profoundly. From a young age, I heard many voices around me at home, school, and church. There were voices of people I knew and those I didn't. Like the voices and sounds I heard with my new cochlear implants, some were good, and some were not. Some made me laugh, some made me cry, and some made me cringe. Voices built me up, and some tore me down.

FALSE MESSAGES GROW LIKE WEEDS

Several of these voices communicated things to me about myself that were not true, and I began to believe them. They became like weeds in the garden of my heart. Weeds in a garden compete with the plants and flowers for light, water, and nutrients and can starve the healthy plants there. The voices communicating lies to my heart began to starve the plants of truth God was trying to grow.

Unlike my cochlear implants, I couldn't shut the voices off, no matter how I tried. They flooded my heart and mind daily. I would put the truth of God in my heart, and the weeds would choke it out. There were messages everywhere from people, television, magazines, church, and random everyday places. Television and magazines showed pictures of perfect women with perfect bodies, hair, and makeup, all shouting, "This is what you need to look like, or no one will ever want you!"

At church, I learned that my worth was tied to how well I behaved or to what extent I made those around me look good or bad. Most people seemed fixated on appearances and surface performances. No one really took the time to care about my heart and what caused me to react or behave a certain way. Their priority was more about changing my behavior and changing me.

People in every area of my life seemed to send the same message: that I wasn't good enough. Many times, this happened because I wasn't just like them: I didn't like what they liked, or I didn't do exactly what they wanted me to do. Some made fun of my hearing and slurred speech, constantly pointing out that I was different, and something was wrong with me. All this created a message that I was invisible and unseen, not valuable or worth protecting, and simply a disappointment.

These messages resonated in my heart and, like seeds, sank deep into the soil of my heart. Without realizing it, the messages grew up like weeds, quick and fierce, destroying the good fruit God was trying to grow. Religion's voice multiplies this message by saying we need to have our lives together all the time. It says to stuff our feelings and prioritize looking good on the outside. Just the thought of trying to be perfect created a lot of pressure, and one way I coped was by creating different masks to wear to hide the real me.

COUNTERFEIT MASKS

I had masks for every person and every occasion. I knew what each person wanted me to be, and I put on the mask for them because the message I believed was that I was not good enough just being me.

I remember being pregnant with my oldest son. I experienced a moment when God opened my eyes to see clearly. He revealed the truth that I had lived like a chameleon, becoming like whoever I spent time with. I became what other people expected, or I tried to be who they wanted me to be, and I had no idea who I was inside.

I was a terribly broken young girl.

I lived in this cycle of trying to be who I needed to be for God and others, putting on the masks, ignoring my pain and woundedness, and trying to be better in my own strength and way. My heart wanted to know God, and I wanted to be what He wanted me to be, too. Religion had painted a picture of what that was, and I didn't know it then, but it was a counterfeit portrait.

This religious cycle wore me out. It was exhausting.

Meanwhile, I was reading God's Word, praying in the way I knew how, and trying to understand this relationship with Jesus.

GOD AT WORK

God began peeling me like an onion, which wasn't easy. I was more like an onion with a crust around it because my walls were so hard and high. Slowly, He exposed the lies and pulled up the roots of those weeds one at a time. Some came out without much of a fight, others got pulled out but grew back up again, and still others wouldn't budge.

What are some of the lies you have believed? How has a religious background made it difficult for you to see yourself as Jesus sees you?

The messages we get used to, whether at church, home, school, or through other people, affect us, and while they are not the truth, they are tough to unlearn.

The Lord and I have had many conversations about my insecurities, both physical and emotional. I've had moments when I put myself down with words, and God gently spoke to my heart and let me know that my words indicated

His creation was bad, ugly, or weird in some way. It was an offense to Him.

I think of God in the Garden of Eden when He sat back and looked at all He created, including the man and woman. "God saw all that He had made, and behold, it was very good. And there was evening and morning, the sixth day" (Gen. 1:31). He didn't just call it good; He called it *exceptionally* good! I would make a comment about myself in a negative way, and God would quietly say to my spirit that I was calling Him a liar. He asked why I couldn't believe what He said was true.

Those small moments carried a big impact. Why is it that when our friends put themselves down, we are right there to speak God's truth to them and encourage them, yet we can't do it for ourselves? Why can't we accept how much God says we are worth to Him? We are worth so much to Him that He sent Jesus to die, to take our sins, flaws, and failures to the cross, so that we might have a right relationship with God.

I am worth that much!

You are worth that much!

RENEWED AND TRANSFORMED

This chapter was thirty years in the making, as my relationship with Jesus renewed my mind and cultivated my heart. The problem with lies and weeds is that sometimes we don't even know they exist. I didn't always realize how false messages were impacting me until they caused significant damage and destroyed the crops God was trying to plant. I have mistaken weeds for flowers so many times. The lies become so real over time that they feel and look like the truth. So I leave the lies in my garden instead of pulling them out. Then deception takes over.

A few years ago, God exposed another layer. He showed me that the lies I believed about being inferior and lacking any potential or worthwhile skills had caused me to build protective barriers around myself. I experienced severe reactions to certain situations because I would go into self-protective mode and defend myself. People said things that weren't meant in the way I heard or received them, but their words triggered deep wounds within me, and I responded harshly. God showed me that the voice sending the message was not always the person in front of me. People may feed the hurt and pain from the message sent by their words, but they don't put it there. God showed me that my reactions sometimes come from the lie that I am living out at that moment.

Responses come from truth. Reactions come from a hurt heart. Responses come from a healed heart.

I had more healing to do. The weeds of lies were still choking the plants of truth in my heart. The voices in my life were still louder than God's voice to me. I began digging deeper, and He began pulling more layers out. The truth of His Word began pulling the roots of those lies.

Religion emphasizes behavior and stresses that your works and what you do are what define you and determine your value. There is nothing like changing seasons to expose this lie.

The season when my children grew up, left home, and became adults spotlighted this lie. In this season, I suddenly realized specific roles, tasks, and jobs were done. I knew I wasn't needed in the same way, and I began feeling lost. The lie that I was not worth as much anymore surfaced at the top of my heart, and my mind found ways to fill the empty spaces and time with more things to do.

God began sharing with me that He did not want me to fill spaces. He wanted me to be with Him for a while without distraction. Jesus told Martha that Mary sitting at His feet, taking in every word He was saying, was the better thing (see Luke 10:41–42).

Why are we so afraid of not having many things to do? Why do we allow this to define our worth?

Religion says that we need to do and then be. A relationship with Jesus says that the doing will come out of the being.

I needed to regroup with the Lord. I needed to seek Him for what the next season would look like at home and church. He was calling me to rest, to be still and know Him better:

> "Be still, and know that I am God. I will be exalted among the nations, I will be exalted in the earth!" (Ps. 46:10 ESV).

In the stillness and the being, God meets us. Will we slow down long enough to meet Him there? It is in the stillness that He exposes the lies. It is in the stillness that healing comes. The enemy of our souls is always looking for a way to resurface the lies and cause the weeds to thrive. He likes to use the noises of this world to drown out God's voice. Even the great prophet Elijah heard God in the smallest whisper:

> And he said, "Go out and stand on the mount before the LORD." And behold, the LORD passed by, and a great and strong wind tore the mountains and broke in pieces the rocks before the LORD, but the LORD was not in the wind. And after the wind, an earthquake, but the LORD was not in the earthquake. And after the earthquake, a fire, but the LORD was not in the fire. And after the fire, the sound of a low whisper. (1 Kings 19:11–12)

God's voice has often come to me through a gentle whisper or a soft nudge in my spirit. I have struggled to hear it among the screaming of lies by the enemy or the sharp pains of the hurt, disappointment, and battles going on inside me. But the more He heals my heart and replaces those lies with His truth, the more I hear the gentle whisper and live in response mode.

God is still healing my heart, but my garden is looking much better. The plants are no longer wilting and are growing stronger and healthier. I am taking off my spiritual cochlear implants to shut off the noises and the multitude of voices around me that threaten to overwhelm me and bring sensory overload. God's voice is getting louder, and the enemy no longer has the same power over me and my heart anymore.

Don't let the voices of religion rob you of knowing who you are in Christ! Let Him replace those lies with His truth and exchange your received messages for His messages. You will exchange depression for hope and anxiety for peace. Watch and experience that pain turning into joy and that self-protective shell melting off.

You will see yourself for the first time through the eyes of Jesus and walk in humble confidence. After walking through this process, I can't begin to describe the beauty I see, and I want to continue moving forward. I want to learn how to live here consistently. There will be times of testing and temptations that try to sway me off the path I'm on. I won't always handle these situations perfectly, but I pray God keeps me moving forward in this truth. My heart desires truth for every person on this earth, and I know it is our heavenly Father's heart, too.

As I sit outside on my patio, I hear the birds singing, hammers banging, and cars and airplanes flying by, but above all—I hear the voice of the Holy Spirit reminding me I am His beloved creation, and I finally trust and believe Him.

Chapter 7:

WATCHING THE RELATIONAL WALLS FALL DOWN

Building forts has always been a favorite activity for me. Growing up, I loved making them out of whatever was available. I used blankets, sheets, beds, boxes, and anything else I could find around the house. I filled my forts with pillows, blankets, stuffed animals, and games, and they became wonderfully comfortable, safe places, where I enjoyed spending time. When my boys were young, they spent lots of time playing with Legos, and we made forts out of those, too. I would build the protective walls in a square or circle shape and stack the Legos as high as I could before they fell down.

One thing I've learned on my spiritual journey is that following religion is quite different from following Jesus. *Merriam-Webster* defines religion as "a personal set or institutionalized system of religious attitudes, beliefs, and practices."[2] Under religion, I followed a set of rules and traditions I thought made me good or acceptable, and I began to build internal forts with high walls.

Religion drives us to achieve perfection and constantly work toward an impossible standard, and when we don't meet it, we feel shamed and condemned. As we live under that standard, we also begin to develop the same standard for others. With our words and actions, we put others in this religious prison with us.

I thought that because an impossible standard was being placed on me, I needed to hold everyone else to the same standard. If religious rules and attitudes measured my Christian life, then they should measure the lives of other people, too. Right?!

VALUING RULES VERSUS VALUING PEOPLE

This mindset and perception trickled down into relationships and devastated them. The problem with that way of thinking and living is it causes the measurement of those relationships to be based on behavior instead of the person and our relationship with them.

When others don't live up to the religious behavioral standards we've formed, then a critical and judgmental attitude arises. Just like the Pharisees, we think, *I'm so glad I'm not like those sinners!* (see Luke 18:10–12). In reality, we are like them because we fail just as often. This critical and judgmental attitude causes pride to grow and walls to build up until there isn't any room for grace. We don't have grace for ourselves or for others.

If we hold onto this mindset and bring it into our marriage or other relationships, failures and mistakes are hard to move past or work through. We may bear grudges, which leads to bitterness and resentment, and we may repeatedly set our spouse (or others) up for failure. In parenting, we can cause our children to feel like their behavior is more important than who they are as people and their hearts. This message communicates that our love is conditional and how we feel about them is based on their behavior and not who they are as a person.

Religion causes us to focus on the behavior first. A relationship with Jesus focuses on the person and the relationship first.

UNCONDITIONAL VERSUS CONDITIONAL LOVE

Religion can be based on conditional love. A relationship with Jesus is always based on His unconditional love for us.

My love for my husband becomes conditional when I live out of a religious mindset. My love for my children becomes conditional when I live in that place. I cause them to feel as though my love for them depends on their behavior, which defines them. This doesn't mean we agree or condone behaviors that are not godly, or we just let them get away with anything they want and allow them to disrespect us as parents, because that is not love. It does mean we love them despite the times they disappoint us. We don't stop loving them because they are in a bad place, struggling with sin, or not being nice at the moment. Their behavior does not determine our love for them. Our love for them comes from who they are.

No one can live up to this religious standard. Trying to make everyone feel like a failure all the time puts the most precious people to me in this prison alongside me. Walls begin to build, and more Legos are put on top, creating higher barriers in the fort. As a result, masks go on, lies are told, and genuine relationships disappear. People become afraid of letting others down and disappointing them, and this fear leads to us feeling as if we're walking on eggshells.

My religious mindset caused me to make the people most dear to me feel the same way I hated feeling: as if they didn't live up to my expectations or had messed up so much that they questioned their worth and my love for them. Thinking about this cycle of legalism makes me pause and cry with great remorse. I have had to repent to God and repent and apologize to my loved ones about this.

FEAR VERSUS FREEDOM

Religion causes us to be self-reliant and self-protective.

I was so afraid my kids would go down the same road I went down and make the same mistakes I made. Because I genuinely wanted to save them from the pain of that path, I made many decisions out of fear instead of prayer and trust in God. Self-reliance took over, because living legalistically can cause us to rely on ourselves instead of God. The enemy plants seeds of doubt in our minds, saying things like He did to Eve in the Garden of Eden (see Gen. 3:4–5).

"Did God really say He would be with you?"

"Did God really say we don't need to be anxious about anything?"

"Did God really say He loves you and your children even more than the sparrows, and look at how He provides for them: how much more would He provide for you?"

The whispers continue and the doubts creep in, inviting fear to take over and control us. We begin to mistrust God and feel as if we can't trust anyone except ourselves.

I was also very self-protective and protective of those I love. What I realized was because I didn't always feel protected over the years, I made it a point to protect myself and people I cared about. Living in religion compounded this behavior and built even higher and thicker walls. I lived in a place where I felt as if I couldn't trust anyone to keep me safe: I had to protect myself. My first reaction was to go into a fort so I could be protected and feel safe when that fearful feeling is triggered. Whispers come, doubts creep in, and fear and anxiety take over when we try to take God's place in our own lives and in the lives of those we love.

FEAR VERSUS PEACE

Religion breeds fear and leads to people-pleasing. A relationship with Jesus brings peace and creates a heart that desires to please God above all.

For a long time, I lived in paralyzing fear. As a person, I was still in that religious place of trying to make up with God for all my messes and failures. I strived for love and acceptance from Him, and I projected that onto my family. When we live in constant fear of disappointing others, we can become people-pleasers. The root of people-pleasing is fear, and when we people-please, then we are no longer seeking to please God. As I look around today, all I hear about are people living in fear, anxiety, and depression. Those are prisons in and of themselves. But Jesus came so we could be free and so we could help others live free. That relationship with Jesus frees us from the fear we have been burdened with as we have lived in that life of religion.

PRISON VERSUS FREEDOM

Religion locks us in prison. A relationship with Jesus opens the prison doors.

As God changed my heart and showed me the prison I was in, with the walls built up to the roof and chains around me everywhere, my relationships began to change. The more I understood God's unconditional love for me and His grace, the more I experienced those new mercies every morning, and the better I loved those around me. Slowly, God began renewing my mind, and one chain after another began to fall off. I started to take one Lego at a time off the walls I had built around me.

As I showed myself more grace, this grace flowed into my relationships with my husband and children. The walls between us began to come down, communication improved, and my family began to see and experience more unconditional love from me.

My children are adults now, and I have had to apologize to them for many past mistakes. I know this process will continue until I go home to be with the Lord. One of my biggest regrets and painful realities is that I did not introduce my children to the Jesus I love and know, the one I have a relationship with now. I showed them the religious version of Jesus, not the Jesus in the Bible.

A FALSE REFLECTION VERSUS THE HEART OF GOD

Religion reflects a false Jesus. A relationship with Jesus reflects the heart of our heavenly Father.

Just like the love I have for my children does not change because of their good or bad behavior, God's love for us is everlasting and unconditional. My husband is a human being just like I am. God created him and loves him just as much as He loves me. We both have flaws and failures. We both seek God, want to grow in Him, and we desire to be more like Jesus.

What my husband does or doesn't do shouldn't change my love for him or make him feel my love is conditional. There is accountability for all of us in our behavior. It isn't a blank slate to act terribly or treat each other incorrectly based on our feelings or because we aren't happy with one another, but it does mean we give each other grace.

CONDEMNATION VERSUS CONVICTION

With religion, there is no grace, only condemnation. A relationship with Jesus brings loving conviction. These are two hugely different things. Condemnation is from the enemy and leads us back into a prison of shame. Conviction comes from the Holy Spirit and leads us to freedom.

We should not live our lives condemning people. When we see things in them that don't seem right or don't line up with God's Word, we pray for them. In closer relationships, God sometimes has us tell them the truth in love and have deeper conversations with them. As my relationship with Jesus grows deeper and I experience His love in tangible ways, it trickles down into my relationships with my husband and children and brings them life.

I wasn't aware of how my misunderstandings about God impacted my family for a long time, but God is incredibly faithful in revealing our hearts to us. God continues to renew my mind; He has restored trust, broken down walls, and opened fort doors. I am thankful that He redeems and restores what the enemy has tried to steal.

Do you have unrealistic expectations of the relationships in your life? Do you hold others to a standard that you can't even meet? Do you love others conditionally?

BUT WHAT ABOUT BOUNDARIES?

I want to express that there are relationships in life where we can love people, but due to the nature of the relationship, boundaries are needed. Placing boundaries on relationships to love people and ourselves well does not mean we love conditionally. We have to make sure our heart is where God wants it to be. I love Jesus's example to us. He had many encounters with people in the Bible. One of my favorites is when He encounters a woman caught in adultery:

> But Jesus went to the Mount of Olives. Early in the morning, He came again into the temple, and all the people were coming to Him, and He sat down and began to teach them. The scribes and the Pharisees brought a woman caught in adultery and having set her in the center of the court, they said to Him, "Teacher, this woman has been caught in adultery, in the very act. Now in the Law, Moses commanded us to stone such women; what then do You say?" They were saying this, testing Him, so that they

> might have grounds for accusing Him. But Jesus stooped down and with His finger wrote on the ground. But when they persisted in asking Him, He straightened up, and said to them, "He who is without sin among you, let him be the first to throw a stone at her." Again He stooped down and wrote on the ground. When they heard it, they began to go out one by one, beginning with the older ones, and He was left alone, and the woman, where she was, in the center of the court. Straightening up, Jesus said to her, "Woman, where are they? Did no one condemn you?" She said, "No one, Lord." And Jesus said, "I do not condemn you, either. Go. From now on sin no more." John 8:1–11

The Pharisees brought a woman to Jesus who was caught in adultery. They proceeded to tell Jesus what the law was in these situations. I can picture Jesus looking over at the woman, seeing into her eyes, and right through to her heart.

He challenged the Pharisees and said whoever was without sin could be the first to throw a stone at her. After everyone left, Jesus talked to the woman. He told her to stop sinning, but He didn't condemn her like the Pharisees wanted him to. I also noticed He didn't speak to her about her sin in front of a bunch of people in the crowd. Instead, He waited until they were alone. Despite her behavior, He loved her and treated her with respect. He cared for her where she was but didn't leave her in her sin.

The beautiful thing about Jesus is He always sees the person first; he takes time to see people, talk to them, and ask them questions. He builds relationships. There are countless examples of His personal interactions with people in the Bible. He also doesn't avoid or ignore talking about sin. He brings conviction and loving redirection to them.

I learn so much from Jesus in how I love and interact with others. His love is not conditional or condemning. He doesn't shun people because they are living in sin; instead, Jesus brings Himself. He brings the gospel, and He brings love, conviction, and a heart to see people free from their sin and living victorious lives.

This is how I want to love my people. This is how a relationship with Jesus changes our relationships. It causes us to see people first and behavior last. His love compels us to bring the people we love to the foot of the cross and love them where they are, just as He loves us where we are. If He calls us to speak the truth in love, He gives us the questions and the words. We rely on Him and not ourselves.

We won't do this perfectly, but we will do it better.

The fort that was built up around my heart is coming down. The walls that were built high are crumbling, the woundedness and feelings of inadequacy in my heart are healing, and I am able to love and live in relationships with others like Jesus more and more each day.

Chapter 8:

FROM THE BUILDING TO THE BODY

I first saw the church through the eyes of a child. Early memories aren't as clear to me, but I vaguely remember my preschool church class teachers and the children I grew up alongside. Our church was an old Baptist church, and where we live in Rhode Island, these churches have an incredible and valuable history. The buildings themselves are prized possessions, and people have even left inheritance money to take care of them.

Needless to say, church buildings are essential, but they shouldn't take priority over the real church—the people. Valuing structures over the congregation was a choice I noticed along my faith journey.

I remember a time when there was an opportunity for ministry, and the opportunity was reviewed at a business meeting. The cost was high, but our church had the money and could afford to pay it. As I listened to the discussion and arguments, the main battle was to preserve money for the church building versus investing in people and ministry. Inevitably, the permanent fund kept its money. The building was safe, but the ministry was left without stewardship.

THE BUILDING

I witnessed new people enter the church, but few members talked to or sat with them if they weren't from that denomination. When a pastor came in and wanted to be more community-focused instead of fostering an isolated community within, he was criticized and eventually kicked out. Nothing seemed more important than the building and the denomination associated with it.

Interestingly enough, that church today is practically lifeless. I pass a beautiful building whose steeple stands tall. This is the building where I grew up, was baptized and married, and where I dedicated my children. It is solemn and dark most of the time.

The outside is beautiful, yet the inside is lifeless and dead.

This is what religion breeds: a beautiful exterior. Everything is maintained and kept together well, while the inside dies a little at a time until life is gone completely. Sometimes, this happens without anyone realizing or noticing. I'm sure people walking by my old church wouldn't know the lifelessness that abides there just by looking at the outside of it.

I found myself much like the church I used to attend. I lived to keep the outside looking good and put together while my insides slowly died.

As I grew up and my childlike perspective was removed, I saw and realized things that made me cringe. I discovered that several people in the congregation were like that building. We went into church looking good, like nothing was wrong in life. We put on our smiles and our good church clothes, and we had all the right answers memorized to give out on request. Only certain people were allowed positions and control, and the focus wasn't really on God.

Few people opened up about themselves or shared about their personal relationship with Jesus. I didn't hear much talk about that at all. Everything seemed very surface-level and focused on church politics.

THE PEOPLE

One of the things I loved about the church were the songs we sang. A favorite was "The Family of God," and my heart longed to be a part of the family this song talked about.

I didn't fully experience this feeling of family, but I longed for it. We weren't encouraged to share our hearts or feelings. I wondered how it was possible to build relationships when we didn't talk about what really mattered. If people were open about their struggles and emotions, others looked at them scornfully. People's feelings weren't taken seriously, and if they dared to share them, these feelings were ignored or dismissed.

Religion keeps those things locked up for fear of ruining an image. A relationship with Jesus unlocks our hearts, freeing us to share with Him and others: "Bear one another's burdens, and thereby fulfill the law of Christ" (Gal. 6:2).

The church shouldn't be a place where sharing struggles and burdens is strange or where sharing victories is a point of competition and comparison. God says that sharing our burdens with one another fulfills Christ's law, "Therefore, confess your sins to one another, and pray for one another so that you may be healed. The effective prayer of a righteous man can accomplish much" (James 5:16).

God says confessing our sins to one another and praying for one another brings healing. When we live with a religious mindset, we rob ourselves and one another of healing, which contributes to our living in bondage instead of freedom. So, I stayed in bondage for a long time. I didn't talk about my feelings. Instead, I stuffed them down deeper and tried to ignore them, just as I had been taught. I figured I would be shut down anyway since that was what usually happened. Then I experienced the deep ache I talked about in chapter 1, and I knew God was telling me there was more to this Christian life; there was more to church. Church was more than a building made up of rules, regulations, and putting on a good face.

LIVING AS THE CHURCH

As my relationship with Christ grew, I prayed for Him to show my husband and me a place where we could experience church in a new way. Eventually, God led us to Christian Hill Community Church.

I want to say right here and now that there is no perfect church. Churches have human beings in them, and there are always things to work out and through, just like in a marriage. The difference is experiencing church through a relationship with Jesus and being someplace where this relationship is the focus.

The journey to a new church has been difficult for me. I had built up walls and was very self-protective. I desired a new way of living together as a body of Christ, but I didn't know what this looked like. This experience is similar to when we grow up saying that we aren't going to be like our parents in specific ways, yet because we come from them, some behaviors show up in our lives, like it or not. We are affected by our surroundings and our environment.

As much as I didn't want to be like what I came from, many things had become part of me along the way. I had barricaded my feelings and hardened my heart. I was also a little raw and deeply untrusting. During this time, I prayed for new friends. I didn't have friends to spend time with, and we didn't have close relationships with people outside of family, but I longed for them.

When we got to Christian Hill, I became involved with women's ministry events and a mom's group, and my kids were in the children's ministry and a youth group. I plugged in, and slowly, I got to know some people. My husband worked there, so he knew the people on staff, and we started hanging out with some of them and their families. A couple of years in, we became deacons, and, shortly after, we became ministry leaders.

GROWING IN THE CHURCH

God uses the places He puts us in to grow and expose us.

I began realizing how God had gifted me in specific ways, just as He gifts every believer. This realization took time because I didn't grow up hearing about the Holy Spirit and spiritual gifts, and I came from a place where only certain people held certain positions. Warm bodies were plugged into average tasks, and the common phrase that "Twenty percent of the people in the church do 80 percent of the work" held true. When people told me the giftings they saw in me and encouraged me in those giftings, their words boosted me up.

These boosts and being given the title of "Leaders of the Deacons" alongside my husband sometimes created a prideful spirit in me. I took on those gifts as my identity, as though they made me good or acceptable to others. My identity became too dependent on what I did instead of who I am as a child of God. I think this is because when we live out of a religious mindset, pride sets in. There is a "look at me" attitude that can arise. But when we live from a relationship with Jesus, a humble confidence comes as we serve in the giftings God has given us through the Holy Spirit.

Sometimes, people are placed in church positions as new believers, but they aren't prepared for the responsibility. Pride takes over, and damage is done. Thankfully, I was not a new believer, and my heart was seeking God in the middle of it all. He was continuing to teach, mold, and grow me. He exposed my heart to me and brought me to repentance for weighting my accomplishments more heavily than who I am in Christ.

Religion puts our identity in what we do. Relationship with Jesus puts our identity in being God's child.

Where is your identity found? Have you been stuck in a religious mindset where what you do or don't do defines who you are, or do you know you are God's child? Are you grounded in that truth? Do you live out of that truth?

I'm asking you these questions because it is vital for us to remind one another of the truth. Otherwise, we effortlessly fall back into a religious way of thinking.

God continues to grow me and my husband as deacons, and we have learned an immeasurable amount about loving God's people with a heart like Jesus. Everyone has their struggles, quirks, weaknesses, and strengths, including us.

LEARNING TO BE PART OF GOD'S FAMILY

I have learned how to have difficult and challenging conversations without getting defensive and going into self-preservation mode. I've learned to rely on the Holy Spirit to teach me how to be a part of the body of Christ. Again, religious mindsets and learned behaviors can creep into this process. One of the things that comes from having a religious mindset is being quick to let everyone else know what they are doing wrong and what they need to do or fix. Yet we aren't willing to look into our own hearts or share our own personal struggles. There are days I still slip into these behaviors, but God is faithful to quickly show me when it is happening so He can help me reroute.

God has brought this Scripture to light for me:

> And He also spoke a parable to them: "A blind man cannot guide a blind man, can he? Will they not both fall into a pit? A pupil is not above his teacher, but everyone, after he has been fully trained, will be like his teacher. Why do you look at the speck that is in your brother's eye but do not notice the log

> that is in your own eye? Or how can you say to your brother, 'Brother, let me take out the speck that is in your eye,' when you yourself do not see the log that is in your own eye? You hypocrite, first take the log out of your own eye, and then you will see clearly to take out the speck that is in your brother's eye." (Luke 6:39–43)

For a long time, I fought with this verse. I felt like it meant I couldn't voice how I felt to someone. I read these verses and filtered them through the frustrations of people not wanting me to talk about my feelings or things that weren't comfortable. I assumed God was shutting me down too. But what God is really saying is that we need to take care of our own hearts first before we go and talk to our brother or sister. It is difficult to see clearly when our lenses are blurry or scratched.

God has taught me to take care of my heart first and be careful that I am not reacting because I'm seeing out of the wrong filter. Instead, He wants me to respond with truth in love. I have to continually examine my heart in this area and discern if my motivation is what it should be.

As I have spent time with different people individually or in ministry groups, I have learned to trust more. God has healed wounds and torn down walls as He has placed sweet sister relationships in my life. I have gained big brothers and beautiful, caring sisters who walk alongside me in life. I have learned what it truly means to live life with a church family and without the fear of being hurt or left.

I have older friends who pour into me and love me as I walk through the seasons they have already been through. I have peers who share similar struggles as we face difficult seasons together and younger friends who are like my own children whom I love and encourage as God gives me the opportunity to do so.

These church family relationships are a gift.

THE CHURCH AS THE BODY OF CHRIST

My relationship with Jesus has shown me that the church is the body of Christ. We need each other. He has, indeed, given me a family.

Religion keeps us holed up and isolated, feeling like we must do this life alone. It causes us to care about our outsides the most because our image is the most important. A relationship with Jesus says His image is the most important, and when we live as the body of Christ and share our struggles and sins with one another, we are healed. We show the world who Jesus is, and we bring Him glory.

Religion is always about us. A relationship with Jesus is about giving God the glory. It is no longer about the building, the outside, or my image. It is now about the body of Christ, my inside, and His image.

And just like the words in that song, "The Family of God," remind us, we are no longer outcasts; because of Jesus we belong.

Be encouraged, God loves you, and you are His. You are a part of the body of Christ, and that is where you belong!

Chapter 9:

BEING BROUGHT BACK TO THE HEART OF WORSHIP

My first memory of the word *worship* was when I saw it printed in bold black letters in the old church bulletin. By now, bulletins are extinct, and some of my younger friends probably won't even know what a paper bulletin is!

At the beginning of the service, there was always a call to worship. Someone would read a Bible verse or a call to worship from the hymnals that sat behind each pew. Right after the reading, we started worship time, which consisted of singing a song from the old brown or green hymnals while someone accompanied us on the piano or the beautiful, ancient organ at the front of the church.

I would get easily distracted while the songs were playing, and my hearing loss didn't help my focus. Unless I knew the song well or liked the words, my mind drifted. In my confused or frustrated state about where we were in the song or how it sounded, my eyes stared blankly at the words on the page or wandered around the room, observing others as they sang.

Mostly, I saw serious, stoic faces and stiff, postured bodies singing the words of the hymns. No one seemed excited about what they were singing. There were exceptions now and again, but not very often.

Like everything else in this Christian life, worship seemed like a ritual or something we did and checked off the list. The focus was more on which hymnal to use and what songs to sing. Oh, there were arguments galore about the hymnals! This was a church-dividing topic. I couldn't wrap my head around why it mattered as much as it did to the people who fought so hard for us to use one hymnal or the other.

THE HEART OF WORSHIP

Looking back, I wonder where Jesus was in all of those arguments. If worship was supposed to be all about Him, it sure didn't seem like it was about Him at all. It became about what people wanted, not what He wanted.

We began singing contemporary songs and hymns when we shifted into the home church. One song in particular got me thinking pretty deeply about all of this. It was called "The Heart of Worship."

I took the words of this song in. They raised my curiosity, and I wanted to know more about what I was singing. Since the song alludes to the fact that the music isn't playing very loudly, I took that to mean that worship was more than just the music and the singing. It sounded like worship was meant for God, not for me. It was something I was bringing to Him.

I wanted to understand what He required, and I got a little scared that He was looking deeper into my heart because my heart felt really messed up.

This sent me on a quest. I wanted to understand more, so I began looking at the Scriptures, and a few stood out to me.

Samuel said, "Has the LORD as much delight in burnt offerings and sacrifices, As in obeying the voice of the LORD? Behold, to obey is better than sacrifice, And to heed than the fat of rams" (1 Sam. 15:22 NKJV).

I didn't find these exact words in only one place. Rather, multiple Scriptures throughout both the Old and New Testaments said the same things, which suggested to me that this truth was important to hear and understand. Here are two other Scriptures that stood out to me:

> For You do not delight in sacrifice, otherwise I would give it; You are not pleased with burnt offering. The sacrifices of God are a broken spirit; A broken and a contrite heart, O God, You will not despise." (Pss. 51:16–17)

> With what shall I come to the LORD And bow myself before the God on high? Shall I come to Him with burnt offerings, With yearling calves? Does the LORD take delight in thousands of rams, In ten thousand rivers of oil? Shall I present my firstborn for my rebellious acts, The fruit of my body for the sin of my soul? He has told you, O man, what is good; And what does the LORD require of you But to do justice, to love kindness, And to walk humbly with your God?" (Mic. 6:6–8)

In these verses, we see that obedience matters to God: a heart that hears and obeys and a broken and contrite heart. This reflects a person who knows their need for Jesus and is willing to admit it, which shows humility. That was what God required, and it was what mattered to Him.

I knew I hadn't been obedient in many things, but my heart wanted to be who God created me to be. I just didn't know how to do that very well.

Religion makes worship about us. A relationship with Jesus creates a heart in us that turns our focus of worship on Him.

MAKING WORSHIP ABOUT JESUS

I wanted to make my worship about Jesus. Before, I'd focused on looking the right way or standing and singing the song like everyone else, but it hadn't meant much to me up to that point. It was just what we did, steps in the process. We sang a few songs before we had communion, and the pastor preached.

No one really talked about what worship was and what it meant. It was either about singing from the proper hymnal or singing a good song. No one spoke about the heart behind it.

I continued seeking God about this and reading more Scriptures about worship and my heart, the heart that God desired me to have. I wondered, *What did having a heart that pleased God look like in real time?*

I loved reading about King David, because he was known as a man after God's own heart. When I read about King David, I see a man who was a sinner just like us. Because of his sin at times, he ended up in some chaotic and complex places, and he suffered severe consequences along the way.

Yet, David was a man after God's heart. What set him apart?

As I read about him, I saw a man with a repentant heart—one who was willing to come before God, admit his sin, and ask for forgiveness sincerely. He lamented over his sin. You see David's love, confidence, and faith in God throughout the Scriptures. He was a man who relied on God and knew his need for God. Until the end of his life, he served and worshipped God.

Religion keeps us in condemnation and shame, so we don't move toward God. A relationship with Jesus brings conviction of our sins so we might draw close to God in repentance and worship.

WORSHIPPING AS THE SPIRIT LEADS

I knew I fell short in many ways, but I longed to worship Him wholeheartedly. I kept seeking God, and when I was convicted, I repented. I practiced drawing close to Him in those moments instead of pulling away in condemnation and shame, as I had done for many years.

There came a time when we were worshipping at a sister church, and I began feeling the urge to raise my hands in worship. I felt the Holy Spirit tugging on my heart to lift my hands during a song. This was new for me! Fear paralyzed me, because no one in this church did that, and I wondered if it might even be offensive. On top of my paralyzing fear, I have severe people-pleasing issues and was panicking about what people would think or say.

The first few times, I ignored it, and I just couldn't get my hands up. My fear kept me frozen in place, unable to move. As I looked around the room, contemplating what was happening, I noticed that my mother-in-law had raised her hands a little bit as well. She didn't seem worried or concerned about the people around who weren't doing it, so I was encouraged to do it anyway.

A song came on shortly after, and I felt the urge to lift my hands again. Sheepishly and slowly, I began to raise my hands in the air. It felt freeing. Something was happening inside me as I allowed myself to be vulnerable and obedient to what God was leading me to do.

It felt like surrender in a new way.

I went home and looked up Scriptures about this. I am sure I had seen it here or there along the way, but not anything that had stood out to me. There are many Scriptures about lifted hands, but one is my favorite: "So I will bless You as long as I live; I will lift up my hands in Your name" (Ps. 63:4).

This whole Psalm is one of my favorites, so I encourage you to read it all, but what I learned was that lifting my hands in worship was pleasing to God. We don't have to raise our hands in order to worship, but it's certainly not wrong to do it. It blesses the Lord. This was another step in my worship journey.

Religion keeps us limited in our worship. A relationship with Jesus frees us to worship in ways the Holy Spirit leads us.

GROWING INTO WORSHIP

There have been many postures in worship over the years as I have grown in my relationship with the Lord. I have learned to pay attention to the words I have been singing, and those old hymns have become precious to me as I understand more about what they mean.

God doesn't want empty words or words we don't mean any more than we wish to hear such words from other people. God doesn't want us to tell Him things we think He wants to hear.

There have been moments over the years when I have been in challenging and tumultuous places in my heart. I have stopped singing in the middle of a song, letting the tears flow and telling God I couldn't sing the words because I didn't mean them. I have had to stop singing the song and be honest with God.

"God is spirit, and those who worship Him must worship in spirit and truth" (John 4:24).

For me, the truth in that moment was I didn't believe the words I was singing, and it was a lie for me to keep singing them. So, instead, my worship was tears flowing in silence while He ministered to me where I was in that time and place. I brought my broken heart to Him; that was the worship He wanted. He didn't want me to sing the song because that was what everyone else was doing at the moment. He wanted me to worship Him in spirit and truth as I brought my broken heart to Him.

Religion says to sing anyway and pretend to be okay. A relationship with Jesus says come as you are.

That is freedom.

To worship is to be brought into God's presence, not just in those moments at church while we sing songs but also in our everyday lives with God:

> "O God, You are my God; I shall seek You earnestly. My soul thirsts for You, my flesh yearns for You, In a dry and weary land where there is no water. Thus I have seen You in the sanctuary, To see Your power and Your glory. Because Your lovingkindness is better than life, My lips will praise You" (Pss. 63:1–3).

I want to bring God my whole heart into worship wherever I am in whatever place I am in, trusting He will meet me there and receive my sacrifice of praise to Him. That is my prayer for you too.

Chapter 10:

LEAVING THE PHARISEE LIFE AND LOVING THOSE LEFT BEHIND

Ever since I was a little girl, I have always had a curious nature. I constantly want to know and understand who I am, the people I love, and those around me. My heart's desire has always been to be seen, known, and loved. We are created to be seen, known, and loved by our heavenly Father and to see, know, and love Him. This is the place where some of my deepest hurts and wounds have lingered. Pains have come from those who haven't seen me or those who have looked at the outside appearance and made assumptions about me without genuinely getting to know me. I've also been wounded by those who have rejected my love.

As I journeyed through the Gospels to explore the Pharisees, I noticed they didn't take time to get to know Jesus. They didn't seek to understand Him or find out who

He was; instead, the Pharisees used what they saw to make assumptions about who Jesus was, and they sought to make others see Jesus the way they saw Him. Most Pharisees didn't seek a real relationship with Jesus. Yet they strictly enforced God's laws and the man-made rules that emerged from those laws—all in God's name.

When you find yourself around people who are mostly concerned with following laws, rules, regulations, and religious traditions, it's difficult not to prioritize what they prioritize. You soon find yourself focused on keeping up appearances and you easily slip into conversations where you criticize and judge others. If you only spend time with people from one denomination or only have friendships with people you're comfortable with, you stop seeing anyone outside that circle. Looking back, I know I fell into many patterns of thinking and behaving because that's what I was around or what I was taught.

As a young Christian, I was like a baby trying to learn how to walk as I navigated this newly restored relationship with Jesus. I had come out of my prodigal time as a chameleon, blending in wherever I went. I had survived this way for years and reentered my relationship with Jesus the same way.

WALKING LIKE A PHARISEE

Several characteristics come with Pharisee-like living, and these characteristics contradict Scripture:

> Do not judge so that you will not be judged. For in the way you judge, you will be judged; by your standard of measure, it will be measured to you. Why

> do you look at the speck that is in your brother's eye but do not notice the log that is in your own eye? Or how can you say to your brother, "Let me take the speck out of your eye," and behold, the log is in your own eye? You hypocrite, first take the log out of your own eye, and then you will see clearly to take the speck out of your brother's eye. (Matt. 7:1–5)

First, Pharisees are overly critical and judgmental. We first must define judgment because this word is often taken out of context and defined incorrectly. *Strong's Concordance* defines judgment as "condemnation, punishment, calling into question, or damning."[3] When we judge in this way, we put ourselves in God's seat, and none of us belongs there. This situation is quite different from a close friend coming to you with concerns about things in your life they think are harmful to you. Too often, God is trying to speak to us through others, and we pass it off as judgment because we are uncomfortable with the conviction that comes with that interaction.

Throughout the Gospels, we see the Pharisees constantly picking apart Jesus's actions. They criticize Jesus at every turn, and they do it in front of people in order to ruin His reputation or discredit Him. We can do that with each other if we have a Pharisee attitude.

Most Pharisees in the Bible don't talk about their own behavior or respond with humility when Jesus exposes their own hearts. Instead, they ignore what Jesus is teaching them, or they seek revenge on Him (Matt. 23:1–36; Matt. 22:41–16; Matt. 15:4–6; Matt. 12:14; Mark 2:23–3:6; Luke 6:1–11; John 5:1–18).

When we behave like Pharisees, we become critical and judgmental in our words and deeds. We try to remove the speck from our brother's eye without being willing to look at and deal with the log in our own eye. If we seek a relationship with Jesus, He exposes our hearts and gives us the strength and wisdom to deal with our own issues so we can better walk alongside others and help them with theirs. Living this way is challenging but necessary if we are going to grow in a healthy relationship with Jesus and others.

The second characteristic of Pharisee-like living is gossipy conversation. I'll never forget when I first heard my own tones in my voice after getting cochlear implants. My husband and I were discussing a topic we were passionate about, and I heard my tone when I said something to him. I was convicted immediately by the Holy Spirit, so I changed my tone and apologized. This incident increased my awareness and helped me realize how I sounded.

The same type of scenario can happen with gossip. *Merriam-Webster* defines a gossip as "a person who habitually reveals personal or sensational facts about others."[4] This is a lifestyle or a habitual action and not an occasional slip. When I hear myself sliding into gossip, my heart becomes heavy because I know that gossip is not how God wants me to treat others. In fact, there are several places in His Word where He shows us this clearly:

> "Women must likewise be dignified, not malicious gossips, but temperate, faithful in all things" (1 Tim. 3:11).

> "O Timothy, guard what has been entrusted to you, avoiding worldly and empty chatter and

> the opposing arguments of what is falsely called 'knowledge'—which some have professed and thus gone astray from the faith" (1 Tim. 6:20–21).
>
> "He who goes about as a slanderer reveals secrets, Therefore do not associate with a gossip" (Prov. 20:19).

God is serious about gossip, and He knows we struggle with it. Because I'm curious, I wanted to understand why the Pharisees consistently gossiped and talked maliciously about Jesus. I believe they were jealous.

Jealousy is often the root of gossip. When we are jealous of someone, we feel superior when we talk about them negatively. By saying things to try and change positive perceptions about a person, we think we can instead influence others to think great things about us. If we listen to gossip, whether from our own mouths or someone else's, we expose the ugliness in our own hearts. Gossip has brought that pinch of conviction, just like that day when I heard my not-so-great tone toward my husband.

For those of us who are people-pleasers, we tend to change ourselves so others see us differently or better, but Jesus didn't do that. He remained true to who He was, and He was faithful to stay on the course His Father set for Him:

> "If you had known what these words mean, 'I desire mercy, not sacrifice,' you would not have condemned the innocent. For the Son of Man is Lord of the Sabbath." Departing from there, He went into their synagogue. And a man was there whose hand was withered. And they questioned Jesus, asking, "Is it lawful to heal on the Sabbath?"—so that they

> might accuse Him. And He said to them, "What man is there among you who has a sheep, and if it falls into a pit on the Sabbath, will he not take hold of it and lift it out? How much more valuable then is a man than a sheep! So then, it is lawful to do good on the Sabbath." Then He said to the man, "Stretch out your hand!" He stretched it out, and it was restored to normal, like the other. But the Pharisees went out and conspired against Him, as to how they might destroy Him. (Matt. 12:7–14)

Jesus infuriated the Pharisees, as you can see. The Pharisees were angry because they couldn't control Jesus. When people feel out of control, they get angry. Anger comes out in many forms. Again, I see Jesus staying steady in who He is and what His Father has called Him to do here on earth. The Pharisees' anger and conspiracies didn't shake or scare Jesus. He stood firm. Jesus knew who He was, and He understood the authority He had, despite how many times the Pharisees questioned that authority.

The Pharisees remained relentless, and throughout the time Jesus lived on earth, they tested Him, questioned His authority, gossiped about Him, and criticized Him and His disciples. Yet He stood firm and never wavered. He spoke the truth and wasn't afraid to communicate it to the Pharisees. Jesus loved the Pharisees. He wanted them to see Him for who He was and be His followers, but He didn't soften things or shy away from speaking firm truth into their lives. He also didn't try to force them to accept Him.

I learn a lot from Jesus.

We can easily get distracted by the reactions and responses of the Pharisees in our lives, but we must keep our eyes on Jesus, the author and perfecter of our faith. We must stay true to who God created us to be and not be swayed away from the course God has put us on earth to live out. The only one who should be in control of us is the Holy Spirit, not the opinions and expectations of others or our insecurities, emotions, or circumstances. Do you know who you are in Christ? Do you know how God has created you? Do you know you have the Holy Spirit living inside you? Do you know the authority and power you have because of that truth?

> However, you are not in the flesh but in the Spirit, if indeed the Spirit of God dwells in you. But if anyone does not have the Spirit of Christ, he does not belong to Him. If Christ is in you, though the body is dead because of sin, yet the Spirit is alive because of righteousness. But if the Spirit of Him who raised Jesus from the dead dwells in you, He who raised Christ Jesus from the dead will also give life to your mortal bodies through His Spirit who dwells in you. (Rom. 8:9–11)

> For God has not given us a spirit of timidity, but of power and love and discipline. (2 Tim. 1:7)

> You are from God, little children, and have overcome them; because greater is He who is in you than he who is in the world. (1 John 4:4)

I don't believe we fully understand that we have the Spirit of the living God inside us, who has the very same power that raised Jesus from the dead. The enemy has no hold on us.

Jesus understood the authority He had, and nothing anyone else said or did changed that truth.

GOING TO EXTREMES

I have had to learn not to go to extremes in almost everything I do. In the past, I followed and went along with what was happening around me—and even joined in—because I felt inferior or fearful of what people would say or do. I wasn't confident in my relationship with Jesus or secure in who I was in Christ. Honestly, I have days where I still struggle with this. By contrast, I can also reach a point where I'm fed up, and I argue, debate, or defend. Jesus doesn't respond in anger or out of frustration. But He also doesn't disguise or soften the truth when He speaks to the Pharisees. He just calmly yet firmly speaks the truth and stands firm in it.

As I sit and ponder these things, I think back to when I was a young girl in school.

As I walked down the hall of the middle school, I searched for the room I needed to get to. I remember walking by a group of kids huddled in a small circle, whispering to one another as they snuck stares my way. One boy began mimicking my nasally speech, which was the result of my hearing loss, and the kids around him quietly giggled. I felt hurt, anger, and fear all at once, and my face turned a shade of red that no one could ignore.

When I read about Jesus and the Pharisees, I often envision them huddled in a group like this, whispering and staring as Jesus walks by or speaks to an individual or a crowd of followers. I imagine them making fun of Jesus as they questioned and challenged His authority in front of the people.

I wonder how Jesus felt. I feel anger and frustration for Jesus. I haven't enjoyed experiencing the challenges, snickering, smudged reputation, and feeling alone because of my relationship with Jesus. Yet, at times in my life, I have also been the one whispering, gossiping, questioning, and challenging others. I have been the critical one and the one who points out a person's weakness, just like that boy did with me.

HEART CHANGE

This relationship with Jesus has changed me. My heart is softened, and many of those wounded places are healed. Just like Jesus exposed the Pharisees' hearts, He has exposed mine. He has shown me when I've had to deal with jealousy in my own heart. He has let me hear the tones in my voice and attitudes, gossip coming out of my mouth, and the questioning of His authority and my authority that comes from Him.

Jesus has taken the fears of being out of control and giv en contentment with Him being in control. He has broken off the bondage of trying to live up to the religious standard and look the part while my insides are crumbling within. Now, I can stand firm in who He is: my rock, refuge, and redeemer. I can rest in who He has created me to be and remember that the power that rose Jesus from the dead is in me. I have authority in Jesus!

When I am confronted or surrounded by Pharisees in my life now, I can be mindful of Jesus's responses:

1. Don't be shaken. Stand firm in tone without arguing or debating out of anger or frustration.
2. Don't engage in critical talk or gossip.
3. Don't shy away from the truth but do speak the truth out of love for the person and, most importantly, love for God.
4. Pray for those struggling with Pharisee-like behavior and for myself as I engage with them.

I encourage you to allow God to examine your heart. Ask Him to expose any Pharisee attitudes in your heart. I pray that God helps us forgive those who intentionally or unintentionally influence us in these behaviors, whether at churches or in our homes. May we learn to live like Jesus and walk in the truth that He lived out before us here on earth. He is our greatest example!

Chapter 11:

THE COST OF FREEDOM TO FOLLOW JESUS

Freedom. This word is used in countless ways. For the teenager, getting a driver's license represents freedom. It can be a night out on the town together as a couple for young parents. On Memorial Day, those who live in the United States are reminded that our democratic and political freedoms have been bought at a price. We see there is a high cost to gaining freedom and a weighty price to keeping it and preserving it.

Strong's Concordance defines freedom in this way: "True Liberty is living as we should, not as we please."[5] This definition feels contradictory to our flesh. We as human beings want to live the way we want to, how we want to, despite how it affects us or those around us. We want to do what feels good and comfortable all the time.

When Adam and Eve were in the garden, they had complete freedom. There was only one tree God told them not to touch, but they had full access to everything else around them, including Himself. The enemy was able to take their eyes off all that and highlight the tree instead. Satan twisted God's words and painted a picture that God was keeping something good from them when He was actually protecting all the freedom they enjoyed in the garden.

Adam and Eve began to question God's heart and motives. They were completely free in every way. They were even walking around naked, for goodness' sake. They could walk and talk with God at any time. Everything was provided for them without having to work themselves to a grave.

God asked them to stay away from only one tree.

As the enemy spoke those deceptive words to her, Eve became fixated on that tree. She wanted it, and she had to have it. So finally, Eve gave in to the temptation and ate the apple. Instead of gaining the freedom and wisdom she thought she would get, she lost most of what she had been given.

The enemy still does this today.

COUNTING THE COST

God has given us His Word, the Bible. He has given us instructions on life and has said no to certain things for us. Just like a good father, He has given us all we need to live life abundantly while putting parameters around those things that are not good or healthy for us. The enemy comes in different ways, chatting it up in our ears and minds. Our eyes become fixated on those things God has told us to stay away from, and we go toward them, indulging in what we think is better for us, and then we find ourselves losing so much.

The freedom Jesus died to give us is that freedom where we get to live as we should and not as we please. Does that mean that God doesn't want us to have good things or not to enjoy our lives? That is what the enemy would like you to think.

"The thief comes only to steal, kill, and destroy; I came that they may have life, and have it abundantly. I am the good shepherd; the good shepherd lays down His life for the sheep" (John 10:10–11).

We see this all around us. The enemy wants to steal and destroy the abundant life Jesus laid down His life to give us. This kills our hearts and our hopes. I have seen it in my life personally, and I still experience the consequences of the times I listened to the enemy's whispers in my ear.

Living an abundant life doesn't mean that life is always wonderful and prosperous. It doesn't mean we won't struggle or battle with different things. There is a cost to following Jesus. Just like there is a cost to preserving and maintaining our democratic and political freedoms here in the United States, there is a cost to preserving our freedom in Christ. The cost looks different for different people in different seasons.

Sometimes, the cost is giving up things that may not be God's best for you, even though they may be good, and He asks you to let them go. For me, that can be letting go of things that are taking the time I need to be using for what God has called me to do instead of spending hours mindlessly roaming through social media or binging on TV or food to avoid what I should be doing.

Other times, the cost means giving up food and drinks that are affecting my health and hindering me from caring for my body as the temple of the Holy Spirit. Or the cost comes in the form of relationships. God may ask me to let go of toxic relationships or to spend less time with those who don't build me up or don't respect the boundaries I have put in place.

The cost can come in the form of persecution for my belief in Jesus and my desire to live for Him. I may need to deal with those who make fun of my faith or think I am stupid for believing it. It can be dealing with arguments or harsh comments about those beliefs and trying to accept that some people won't like me for that reason alone.

Sometimes, the cost means guarding my heart and mind by not watching certain movies, listening to specific music, engaging in gossipy conversations, or wearing particular clothes. These things can put me on the outside of some friend groups, which is hard for a woman who struggles with stings of rejection and who has lived most of her life trying to fit in.

THE TWO HEART LENSES OF OBEDIENCE

Obedience to God can be lived out through two different heart lenses. The first one is the heart lens of religion. This is the one I lived out of for more years than I would like to admit. Unfortunately, obedience lived through this heart lens does not bring freedom; instead, it brings bondage and puts us in a vicious cycle that either makes us want to jump off this ride or causes us to die inside.

Obedience to God through the heart lens of religion leads us into:

1. A Life of Bondage to Perfectionism

As we try to follow perfectly all that God tells us, we soon realize it is impossible for us as human beings to live life perfectly. Perfectionism leads to condemnation and shame. We have no grace for ourselves or others, and we continue striving to be perfect in our own strength and might. The cycle will continue, and we will live in condemnation and shame with no way out if we continue on that hamster wheel.

Growing up, I had experiences with several very controlling authority figures, and I began to see God the same way. If I didn't obey or behave the way someone told me or expected me to, or if I made a mistake and didn't do things perfectly, someone would point it out, and sometimes the consequences were humiliating. When others are around when this type of criticism happens, such as in a classroom, a store, or at an event, it leaves scars and makes us want to do everything we can to keep those experiences from happening again. Self-protective walls begin to build, and we start obeying simply to please or appease. The cycle of striving begins.

2. A Life of Bondage to Fear

Obedience to God through the heart lens of religion also leads to bondage to fear. We're afraid of failure or messing up. We fear what people will say, think, or do to us if we don't do things right. We become people-pleasers. We become afraid God will punish us, and we panic thinking that God will cause bad things to happen to us because we aren't doing what we are supposed to be doing perfectly.

Living in fear is not freedom; it is bondage. I have lived in crippling and paralyzing fear for most of my life. I would find myself lying to avoid trouble because I was afraid of someone being angry with me, or I was stressed about the consequences that might come to me if I told the truth. I had an unbearable fear of being a terrible wife and mother if I didn't do things well or exactly right. I lived in a debilitating fear of disappointing those I love, especially God. That is not freedom.

3. A Life of Bondage to Pride

I think back to the Scripture in Luke 18 in the parable where the Pharisee is praying to God and thanking Him he is not like other people. In his prayer, he is actually placing himself above people like swindlers, adulterers, or tax collectors. When we obey through the heart lens of religion, it causes us to puff up with pride because we followed the law, checked something off the checklist, or even just lived out some legalistic tradition. Somehow, that suddenly means we are better than other people who haven't. This type of thinking is not freedom for us or others.

I have lived this way. I look back and remember the days when I would live in obedience to one or two things God was telling me, and, somehow, that made me feel better about myself and made me think I had a license to go and criticize where someone else wasn't doing what I was doing. I was quick to judge and tear down others because somehow, in my mind, I had achieved some level of holiness that day by the things I did right. Meanwhile, I know there were many things I was still learning and not hitting the mark on.

Such an attitude and way of living causes other people to see God through a religious lens, and many people who have walked away from God would say that is one of the reasons why they don't want anything to do with God. Pride causes us to be a stumbling block to ourselves and others around us.

However, there is another heart lens to obey through that brings true freedom. That is the heart lens of a relationship with Jesus.

Obedience through the heart lens of a relationship with Jesus leads us into:

1. A Life of Grace

One of my favorite verses is 2 Corinthians 12:9: "He has said to me, 'My grace is sufficient for you, for power is perfected in weakness. Most gladly, therefore, I will rather boast about my weaknesses so that the power of Christ may dwell in me.'"

One of my first steps toward true freedom was the day I realized and understood that perfection is impossible. The Old Testament shows us that we can't live a perfect life, revealing our need for a Savior, Jesus Christ. Our sin separated us from God, and perfection was lost the day Adam and Eve ate the fruit in the Garden of Eden. Since that day of personal revelation, it has been a process of renewing my mind away from that religious thinking that I could live a Christian life by my own strength and power. There have been days when I have gone to God asking why I am so weary, and He gently shows me it is because I am trying to do it all on my own in my strength. He encourages me to stop striving, to be still, know He is God, and live in His grace. To allow Him to be my strength in my weakness. Living that way gives me grace for myself and those around me. That is Freedom!

2. A Life of Faith

Faith is the opposite of fear. When I live in obedience to God through the heart lens of a relationship with Jesus, I can live in faith instead of fear! Faith involves trust. Because of my many other experiences with other human beings who are not trustworthy, I have struggled to trust God fully.

I have been afraid that He had left me alone and wasn't with me during different seasons. I had been fearful that He wasn't protecting me or had my back in certain situations and circumstances. But slowly, I learned to trust Him more and more. I learned to stop, pause, and release my anxieties, cares, and burdens to Him. Fear no longer had control over me most of the time.

Trust has been a work in progress for me. I do believe and trust His love for me, yet there are days when I still doubt that what I am experiencing could be His best for me. There will never be perfection in this until we go home with Him. But He has proven His goodness to me repeatedly in His personal faithfulness to me, and my prayer is to live this verse out in my life:

"When I am afraid, I will put my trust in You. In God whose word I praise, In God I have put my trust; I shall not be afraid. What can mere man do to me?" (Pss. 56:3–4).

That *is* freedom!

3. A Life of Humility

Over the years since I was a woman with that prideful heart, God has renewed my mind and given me His eyes to see myself and others through His.

We are all the same.

We are all created by God and loved by Him.

We come into the same world, born into sin, needing the same Savior.

We all have personal experiences that have wounded us and left us with broken hearts in different ways.

We have the same enemy, Satan, who has whispered the same lies to us about ourselves, others, and God.

Jesus died for *all* of us.

When I begin to see not just other people, but myself, as someone God created and loves enough to die for, it changes my heart lens.

SEEING THROUGH A NEW LENS

When I began to see and understand how God had loved me all of my life, it changed my heart and made me want to stop and pause before I said a critical or judgmental word or walked on the other side of the street or the next aisle in the grocery store to avoid someone.

This is the heart lens that makes me want to reach out to the lonely girl or the one who is lost and wandering. My heart now wants others to experience the same love and hope I have experienced in my relationship with Jesus. It is the same love that loves the sinner yet hates the sin. I want to love with the truth that God has loved me with, the truth He put in my heart that has changed me and set me free in the truest sense of the word. First Peter 5:6–7 says, "Therefore humble yourselves under the mighty hand of God, that he may exalt you at the proper time, casting all your anxiety on Him, because He cares for you."

Pride causes us to lift ourselves up, but God says it is not our job to lift ourselves up, and it's not our job to talk down to others as though we think we are better than them. Instead, God says to humble ourselves and live a life of humility, and He will exalt us in His time. This is freedom!

There is a weighty cost to freedom some days. Our pride or feelings may be hurt, but if we live in obedience through that heart lens of a relationship with Jesus, we honor the sacrifice Jesus paid. The freedom we gain is incomparable to anything we have ever experienced before, and God promises to lift us up and exalt us in due time.

Chapter 12:

MOVING FORWARD WITH A TRANSFORMED HEART

We've all heard the saying "Two steps forward, one step back," and this saying describes how I've felt as I've gone deeper in my relationship with Jesus. I make steps forward in trust and faith, then doubts come, or I fall into believing a lie the enemy throws my way. I allow insecurity and inner turmoil to mess with my forward steps. Other times, those old religious, legalistic attitudes, and mindsets reappear in my thoughts, heart, or conversations.

As God has brought me through this transformation, a verse that sticks with me as a holy reminder is found in Galatians 5:1: "It was for freedom that Christ set us free; therefore, keep standing firm and do not be subject again to a yoke of slavery." Galatians has revealed the transforming power of my relationship with Jesus in my life, and I don't ever want to go back to living a life of religion. I want to keep moving forward as God continues transforming my mind, heart, and life.

As a teenager, I smoked cigarettes for a couple of years. I quit soon after I found out I was pregnant with my son. Back then, you could still smoke in coffee shops and restaurants. I remember being around the smell of smoke after I tried to quit. At first it was hard and tempting. The smell drew me in, and I wanted to grab a cigarette again. After a while, the smell annoyed me, and I felt frustrated and angry around it. Years later, the smell simply bothered me, and I couldn't stand to be around it; I had to get away from it.

This is what it has been like for me transitioning from that life of religion. At the beginning of the transition, being around religious and legalistic places lured me in to take those steps back into former habits or tempted me to step back into old conversations. As time went on, I felt frustrated and angry when I was around those places and behaving in the old ways. When I remembered the places of bondage and pain I used to live in because of religion and legalism, I was angry and determined not to go back to that way of living.

Now, when I am around these places, I can engage for a short time, and then I need to get away from it. I can't be in the smoke of it too long. I don't ever want to go back to that yoke of bondage ever again. I want to keep living free.

LIVING FREE

How do we do this? How do we move forward with this transformed heart? There have been some critical steps for me along the way that I want to share with you.

The first is forgiveness. I have had to forgive those who had a part in teaching me that the life of religion was the way to live. These were people who influenced me to live legalistically or taught me to stuff my feelings down and ignore them. They were negative, critical, and judgmental and made me question what I was hearing from God. Sometimes they drowned out His voice in my life saying they knew better, and I didn't.

This isn't a blame game or me not taking responsibility for my actions, but the reality is we influence each other, and the truth is we are taught by those around us and in authority over us. God holds us accountable for our part in it. I have asked for God's forgiveness for the ways I have influenced others around me this manner, including my children and anyone else along the way. I needed to ask their forgiveness and take responsibility for my part in teaching them that a life of religion is how we should live instead of through a relationship with Jesus. Unforgiveness will keep us in prison, and we will not be able to move forward until we forgive.

The second step I've taken to move forward is to remember that I am not alone, and God is not asking me to do these things in my own strength. He is asking me to trust Him with my whole heart and let Him be the one who does the work. Whenever I have gotten stuck or weary, it has been because I have been trying to do it all myself or be the fixer.

This is hard to do because it means giving God *all* of my feelings and vulnerable thoughts. It means just praying sometimes and not doing anything but waiting. It means dying to my flesh when I want to run or choose the way that's more comfortable.

It is a complete surrender, not a partial one.

COMPLETE SURRENDER

I remember one day when God was speaking to me about this. I was wrestling with some feelings and trying to understand what God wanted from me. He gave me a vision of me hanging off the top of a cliff by my pinky. God's hands cupped underneath me, ready to catch me, encouraging me to let go. Letting go completely was my answer, but I was afraid to do it. The fear and anxiety paralyzed me to stay there hanging by my pinky.

Time passed, and I continued to hold on by a pinky because somehow, I figured I could surrender 99 percent and feel like I still had a tiny ounce of control just in case God didn't come through. So I continued holding on by my pinky, becoming weary as I hung there. Complete surrender and trust were battles I had to fight.

Eventually, I let go, but it was a challenging process that eventually brought more freedom and peace than I could ever have imagined. It strengthened my relationship with Jesus and helped me move forward.

The third step is to remember that my weaknesses are not disqualifiers. In a life of religion, weaknesses are hidden because they represent imperfection. But in our relationship with Jesus, He becomes our strength in our weaknesses; through those weaknesses, God makes Himself known and is glorified.

> And He has said to me, "My grace is sufficient for you, for power is perfected in weakness." Most gladly, therefore, I will rather boast about my weaknesses so that the power of Christ may dwell in me. Therefore I am well content with weaknesses, with insults, with distresses, with persecutions, with difficulties, for Christ's sake; for when I am weak, then I am strong. (2 Cor. 12:9–10)

My hearing loss has felt like such a weakness at times. The limitations and struggles that come with it and the way it separates me from people sometimes is a discouragement, but He has been my strength in it and through it, even in my times of struggle and doubt. He has provided tools for me through my cochlear implants, my audiologist and hearing therapists, and a husband who signs to me when my cochlear implants are off and helps me feel included when I am struggling. God has given me friends who love me well in it, even when it is frustrating.

My simplemindedness has felt like a weakness, but He pours His wisdom in, and you have to know it doesn't come from me. He fills in my missing links, as I call them. The Holy Spirit truly is my helper.

My personal battles have felt like weaknesses, but as He transforms and heals my heart, He is made known. None of it is anything I could ever do on my own. He is patient and loves me, with a stern kick in the pants every now and again. He is a good Father and a faithful friend.

Matthew West sings a song called "The God Who Stays." The words to this song cause my heart to overflow with gratitude for God who has continually stayed by my side, even when it hasn't felt like it and even when no one else has been there. Even when I walked away from Him because I didn't believe He was there. He has indeed been my strength despite my weakness all the way through, and I know He always will be.

The fourth step I have had to learn to keep moving forward is how to keep my eyes on Jesus daily. I often think of Peter with this one.

> Peter said to Him, "Lord, if it is You, command me to come to You on the water." And He said, "Come!" And Peter got out of the boat and walked on the water and came toward Jesus. But seeing the wind, he became frightened, and beginning to sink, he cried out, "Lord, save me!" Immediately Jesus stretched out His hand and took hold of him, and said to him, "You of little faith, why did you doubt?" (Matt. 14:28–31)

I remind myself of Peter. I am excited and focused, and then as I am walking, I see the wind, rain, and storms around me, and my eyes go off of Jesus and onto the storm. The fears and anxieties kick in, and there I start going down. Jesus stretches out His hand to grab me up.

I am learning not to be so distracted by the storms, but it is difficult sometimes. This is where I put into practice the new mindsets and ways of living through my relationship with Jesus. I talk to Him about my fears and anxieties. I give Him what frustrates me and makes me angry, and I trust that He cares about my heart. I believe that He is walking with me and has good plans for me, and He will eventually use it all for my good and His glory. In the moments I struggle to believe it, I tell Him that too.

There was a hymn I loved growing up, but I never quite understood its meaning. After living through some of this transformation, I understand it much better. The first verse and chorus go like this:

"O soul, are you weary and troubled
No light in the darkness you see
There's light for a look at the Savior
And life more abundant and free
Turn your eyes upon Jesus
Look full in his wonderful face
And the things of earth will grow strangely dim
In the light of his glory and grace."[6]

I am amazed at how when I turn my eyes toward Jesus, as I give Him the storms, the cares, the anxieties, and fears, His peace comes like a flood over me. The enemy tempts me to look around and tries to shake me up, but when my eyes are focused on Jesus, He brings calm to my storms. Isaiah 26:3 puts it like this: "The steadfast of mind You will keep in perfect peace, because he trusts in You."

As I move forward with this transformed heart, I need to keep my eyes on Jesus moment by moment so I don't take those steps back and be tempted to deal with the storms myself. This is intentional. When I feel my thoughts drifting and my eyes shifting, I have to pause and take a moment to give those things to God. I have to surrender the situations and people to Him. I must let Him lead me in how to walk life out here. When I stop and do that, His peace comes, and the anxieties and stresses are not the controlling factors anymore. That is how I want to live going forward.

KEEPING MY EYES ON THE PRIZE

The last step I've taken to keep moving forward in my relationship with Jesus is captured in this verse:

> Not that I have already obtained it or have already become perfect, but I press on so that I may lay hold of that for which also I was laid hold of by Christ Jesus. Brethren, I do not regard myself as having laid hold of it yet, but one thing I do: forgetting what lies behind and reaching forward to what lies ahead, I press on toward the goal for the prize of the upward call of God in Christ Jesus. (Phil. 3:12–14)

As we forgive and let go of the past to move forward, we must focus our eyes ahead. Satan wants to keep us stuck in the past one way or another. Here Paul tells us we need to forget what lies behind. This doesn't happen in a day. Even when we forgive and grieve in order to let the past go, there will be temptations to keep looking back, like with Lot's wife. When those moments hit, feelings rise to the surface, and pain twinges our hearts. We just have to keep bringing these feelings to Jesus. We give them to Him, cry with Him, sit with Him, and let His peace wash over us.

One day it will be easier than it was before if we keep walking toward God one step at a time and what He has for us ahead.

> Therefore, since we have so great a cloud of witnesses surrounding us, let us also lay aside every encumbrance and the sin which so easily entangles us, and let us run with endurance the race that is set before us, fixing our eyes on Jesus, the author, and perfecter of faith, who for the joy set before Him

> endured the cross, despising the shame, and has sat down at the right hand of the throne of God. (Heb. 12:1–2)

We lay aside everything that hinders us and keeps us entangled. The thoughts and things that distract us and detour us. The enemy wants us tied in knots, stuck in our grief and pain, so we won't walk forward in all He has planned for us. Jesus knows what we are going through and can empathize with us as we run this race. When we keep our eyes on Him, we see that He is right there beside us, running with us.

> Let us hold fast the confession of our hope without wavering, for He who promised is faithful; and let us consider how to stimulate one another to love and good deeds, not forsaking our own assembling together, as is the habit of some, but encouraging one another; and all the more as you see the day drawing near. (Heb. 10:23–25)

He has given us one another to encourage and cheer us on as we run. He has also given us one another to help us hold fast to this confession of our hope without wavering.

I pray that as you move forward from here, Jesus becomes more real to you, that where you may have been stuck, you will take Jesus's hand that is reaching out to you. Where there was fear and anxiety, there will be peace. I pray that where there was depression, there will be hope; where there was discouragement, there will be encouragement; and may you know you are not walking through this life alone.

ACKNOWLEDGMENTS

Writing this book has been a journey, and I want to take time to acknowledge those who have walked it with me and have been a part of helping make it happen.

To my husband, Duane, who has supported me in so many ways, making it possible for me to do this. Thank you for encouraging me, loving me, and helping me see this dream become reality. I love and appreciate you!

To my son Kyle, who made me a mama. You are one of God's sweetest gifts to me. You have lived through so much of this with me. Thank you for loving me through the hard times, for always encouraging me in life, and for being there as I wrote this book. I will always be grateful God gave you to me. I am so proud to be your mom. I love you!

To my son David. You are such a gift to me. You too have lived through a lot of this with me. Thank you for your love, prayers, and words of encouragement as I have gone through the process of writing this book. I am forever grateful God gave you to me to be your mom. I love you!

To my sweet sisters in Christ who have prayed me through this process. Thank you for your love, prayers, and consistent encouragement to see this to completion.

To my small group girls who have prayed for me, encouraged me, and cheered me on. You are a gift to me, and I love and appreciate you!

To my online writing friends—the ones I have connected with through the Proverbs 31 Compel program—and others along the way, you have been constant friends, and I have learned so much from all of you. It has been a joy to be on this writing journey with you.

To my content editor, Peggy Bodde, you have taught me an incredible amount about editing and this process. Thank you for helping me with this book. You have been a gift and become a dear friend.

To Shane Crabtree and Carpenter's Son Publishing, what a joy it has been to work with you!

To my readers and those who will pick up this book, thank you for your love and support. I pray as you read these words, Jesus will become personal and real to you and that He will transform your life in ways you never thought possible.

ABOUT THE AUTHOR

Desiree Taylor is a strong Christian woman, writer, and speaker whose focus is to love women and to use the words God has given her to help them connect with Jesus personally—the only One who brings life-changing transformation. Her desire is to walk alongside women, no matter what season they are in, both face to face and online together while journeying toward Heaven.

When she is not writing, she invests her time mentoring and discipling young adult women, serving in Women's Ministry, or finding ways to advocate not only for deaf and hard of hearing people like herself but also for others with special needs.

Desiree resides in Westerly, Rhode Island, with her husband, Duane. They have two adult sons, Kyle and David. In her free time, she loves spending time with family and friends, reading and journaling, or exploring new experiences.

You can find her at www.arenewedcreation.com. She is also on Instagram, Threads, LinkedIn, and Pinterest.

NOTES

1. *Merriam-Webster,* s.v. "Pharisee," accessed December 22, 2023, https://www.merriam-webster.com/dictionary/pharisee.

2. *Merriam-Webster,* s.v. "religion," accessed November 1, 2023, https://www.merriam-webster.com/dictionary/religion.

3. Bible Hub, "Strong's H4941 – mishpat," https://biblehub.com/hebrew/4941.htm.

4. *Merriam-Webster,* s.v. "gossip," https://www.merriam-webster.com/dictionary/gossip.

5. Bible Hub, "Strong's G1657 – eleutheria," https://biblehub.com/greek/1657.htm.

6. Lemmel, Helen H., "Turn Your Eyes Upon Jesus," 1922, accessed January 15, 2024, https://hymnary.org/text/o_soul_are_you_weary_and_troubled.